*TWAYNE'S WORLD AUTHORS SERIES*

*A Survey of the World's Literature*

Sylvia E. Bowman, Indiana University

**GENERAL EDITOR**

# LATIN LITERATURE

Philip Levine, University of California

**EDITOR**

## Quintilian

*(TWAS 59)*

## TWAYNE'S WORLD AUTHORS SERIES (TWAS)

*The purpose of TWAS is to survey the major writers
—novelists, dramatists, historians, poets, philosophers,
and critics—of the nations of the world. Among the
national literatures covered are those of Australia,
Canada, China, Eastern Europe, France, Germany,
Greece, Italy, Japan, Latin America, New Zealand,
Poland, Russia, Scandinavia, Spain, and the African
nations, as well as Hebrew, Yiddish, and Latin Classical literature. This survey is complemented by
Twayne's United States Authors Series and
English Authors Series.*

*The intent of each volume in these series is to present
a critical-analytical study of the works of the writer;
to include biographical and historical material that
may be necessary for understanding, appreciation,
and critical appraisal of the writer; and to present all
material in clear, concise English—but not to vitiate
the scholarly content of the work by doing so.*

# Quintilian

By GEORGE KENNEDY

*University of North Carolina*

Twayne Publishers, Inc.    ::    New York

viro bono docendi perito

Houardo Comfort

QUINTILIAN'S SCHOOL

# Preface

In grave Quintilian's copious work we find
    The justest rules and clearest method join'd.
Thus useful arms in magazines we place,
    All ranged in order, and disposed with grace;
But less to please the eye than arm the hand,
    Still fit for use, and ready at command.
           Alexander Pope, *An Essay on Criticism,*
                Pt. III, 110–15.

This book is an attempt to present and analyze Quintilian's copious work with the thought that a better knowledge of it may be useful to students and teachers of education, rhetoric, and criticism, and to those interested in Roman intellectual and literary history. No general book on Quintilian has ever been published in English, and even the European studies of him have largely been devoted to some special topic such as his sources, his educational system, or his influence. In brief compass I have discussed these, but also Quintilian himself, his times, the organization of his work, and his goal and ideals, and I have most of all aimed at a clear exposition of his thought and a just estimate of his achievement. A great deal more could be said, but I think it would not change the essential picture. Though neither a great writer nor a great thinker, he emerges, to my mind, as a significant, interesting, and appealing figure, and I regret the need now to move on from study of him to other work.

The original call for this book came from my sometime teacher, former colleague, and continued friend Philip Levine, who has made a number of sound suggestions for its improvement. I am also indebted for several perceptive comments to students in my Quintilian seminar at the University of North Carolina.

GEORGE KENNEDY

*Chapel Hill, N. C.*

## QUINTILIAN

### by

### GEORGE KENNEDY

Quintilian was a teacher and critic of
the first century A.D. whose importance
in the history of education and rhetoric
has long been recognized. However, until
now, no general study of his work has
appeared in English. This book in
Twayne's World Authors Series is intended to satisfy that need. In this volume, Quintilian is authoritatively placed
within the framework of history and
thought of his times. His surviving work
is evaluated, and his influence on later
times is traced.

# Contents

# Chronology

# CHAPTER 1

## Quintilian's Background and Career

MARCUS Fabius Quintilianus was an orator and teacher of the early Roman Empire, known principally for a single large work, *De Institutione Oratoria* or *On the Education of the Orator*. The *Institutio*, as the work may conveniently be called, is a compendium of ancient theories on rhetoric and on education. Nothing else tells us so much about what went on in ancient schools or about the objectives at which ancient education aimed. Other authors, Plato, for example, describe ideal educational systems; Quintilian describes schools as they existed through most of Hellenistic and Roman times, with comments and suggestions growing out of his own experience. These schools were principally concerned with rhetoric, and more than half of the *Institutio* is thus an account of rhetoric, the art of persuasion, as it had developed through the contributions of Greek sophists and philosophers, Hellenistic teachers, and Romans, among them Quintilian himself.

Quintilian is interested in producing a perfect orator and in keeping him at the peak of his form. He thus advises on almost everything from the time to initiate studies to the time to retire. An orator as the goal of all education is initially startling to some modern readers, and to understand Quintilian, it is essential first to appreciate what the classical world meant by an orator, why oratory occupied such a central place in literature, and why rhetoric, the theoretical study of oratory, had come to be the backbone of education.[1]

### I  *The Role of the Ancient Orator*

In early Greek culture there were two areas for effective human action: speech and war. The best man was good at both; thus in the *Iliad* Phoenix taught Achilles to be a doer of deeds and a speaker of words. Old men like Nestor, as they lost great physical prowess, might hope to gain greater repute as speakers; Odysseus, though an able fighter, was most famous for his wily words. Speech was the characteristic act of the man of affairs in time of peace: it was the concrete manifestation of what the modern world might label administrative ability, experience, knowledge of the world, or prestige, and it found expression in the councils of state, in legal disputes, and in attempts to influence the will of others both publicly and privately.

As the city states developed and there was less room for the hero at arms, the speaker of words became the commoner type of influential man: thus the orator is an increasingly dominant aspect of the tyrant, the democratic statesman, and the demagogue. He speaks in the assembly; he takes a leading part in the courts; he uses his connections for commercial gain. Greek society was predominantly oral: speech was the principal medium of government, law, and business. Although literacy steadily increased, as did the keeping of records, the use of secretaries, and the amount of correspondence, classical civilization preserved most of its oral basis until the end. Even under the efficient Romans there was only the roughest form of postal service, and of course no mechanical aids to writing, no printing, no typewriter, though systems of shorthand were known. Speech thus remained the fundamental human action. It was in speech that man semed most to excel the brutes, to influence events, to calm the passions, to express his intelligence. There are many eulogies of speech in ancient literature. Quintilian's own version reads as follows:

Will anyone have the hardihood to deny that the famous blind Appius broke off the shameful peace with Pyrrhus by his powers of speaking? Or was not the divine eloquence of M. Cicero admired by the people even when directed against the agrarian laws, and did it not crush the audacity of Catiline and win for himself, though a civilian, public thanksgivings, which are the greatest honor given to victorious leaders in war? Is it not true that oratory has often recalled the terrified minds of soldiers from their fear and convinced those entering the manifold dangers of fighting that glory is preferable to life? Nor does the example of the Lacedaemonians and Athenians move me more than the Roman people, among whom there has always been the greatest honor to orators. I, for my part, believe that the founders of cities would not in any other way have brought it about that what was a wandering multitude should come together to form a people if it had not been stirred by a voice taught to persuade; nor could lawgivers, without the most highly developed power of pleading, have secured that men bind themselves to obedience to law. Even the very codes of human life, naturally honorable as they are, have greater power to form men's minds when the splendor of speech gives a glow to the beauty of the subject. (II,xvi,7–10)

If speech is the characteristic human action, the best orator will be the best man. The goal is not quite open to all; it replaced the hero at arms and was originally aristocratic, but it became possible for someone to rise by ability and luck. Quintilian agreed with many of his predecessors that three things were generally necessary: nature, practice, and art. One had to be born with a certain something, and in the right place, at the right time. Native ability could go a long way, especially if supported by wealth, high birth, moral force, or determination, but in Quintilian's view study was necessary for real perfection. Practice meant self-consciousness and expert criticism. Art meant education, attending lectures, studying books, and learning the system. Both practice and art took teachers, time, and money, but these could be afforded by the future leaders of the state.

## II  *The Study of Rhetoric*

Greek statesmen of the classical period were usually called *rhetores*, "orators." Their principal formal teachers were the sophists, who delivered, for pay, speeches to show what could be done with words, how arguments could be molded and refuted, how subjects could be amplified or compressed, how material could be organized, how style could be adorned. Some sophists had more theoretical interests and composed short treatises on the art of speaking, or aspects of it. The most famous of the teachers of speech in the fourth century was Isocrates, whose school antedated and rivaled Plato's Academy. Isocrates himself regarded his ideal as more worthwhile than Plato's, his subjects as more practical than the hairsplitting subtleties studied with his rival. Aristotle combined both curricula. Nothing that could be studied was beneath his notice, and rhetoric was a useful art.

In the following centuries in Greece, an educational system was developed which taught young children to read and write, and then sent them to a grammar school for study primarily of language and literature; instruction in geometry and astronomy was sometimes available too, and boys could learn music and gymnastics, but only from special teachers. As adolescents, students then moved to the school of a rhetorician. Rhetorical studies had five parts: invention (which included argumentation), arrangement, prose style (including the study of words and their combination), techniques of memorization, and delivery, which involved voice control and gesture. Sets of exercises in composition and expression were developed. Subjects might be general, called *theses* and resembling philosophical arguments, or specific, resembling deliberative or judicial speeches. The latter were declamations and were called *suasoriae* if the orator pretended to give advice in some historical situation, for example, if he urged Alexander to turn back after reaching India, or *controversiae* if the orator spoke in an imaginary court case. Although education was originally a private matter, by Hellenistic times many Greek states had come to supervise the operation of schools.[2]

The Romans came into contact with Greek rhetorical education and practice in the third century B.C.[3] Their own counterpart to the *rhetor* was the *patron*, an aristocrat with social and moral responsibilities for the legal protection of his clients, who were citizens of inferior rank. *Patronus* remained the word for a pleader in a Roman court. At first, the artistic and intellectual qualities of the patron-orator were not stressed at Rome; his personal authority and moral qualities were more important, as was his need for some familiarity with the law. The third century B.C. brought the Romans into Greek-speaking southern Italy and Sicily. The second century brought them into Greece itself, and more important it brought Greek orators, as ambassadors, in great numbers to Rome. Late in the third century Romans began to be praised for their oratorical ability; in the second century oratory had reached a literary level and Cato the Elder thought it worthwhile to publish some of his speeches. Meanwhile, Greek rhetoricians lectured in Rome and Greek grammarians were engaged to teach Romans. By the first century rhetoric was a regular part of education, though schools at Rome remained private institutions.

In early Greece the antithesis of the orator had been the man of action, the soldier. From the time of Plato, the contrast was apt to be drawn in the other direction, with the man of pure speculation, the philosopher. A dispute between rhetoric and philosophy repeatedly burst out. Most Romans preferred the power of the orator, the utility of his art, the relative attainability of his ideal. There were great Roman orators; there is hardly a great Roman philosopher. In fact, with the exception perhaps of the rough soldier, Marius, the great Roman statesmen of the late republic and early empire were all distinguished orators: Cato, the younger Scipio, the Gracchi,

Livius Drusus, Sulla, Cicero of course, Caesar, Pompey, Crassus, Mark Antony, several emperors, especially Augustus and Gaius. In Quintilian's praise of oratory just quoted, it should be noticed how speech is made the tool of the military commander and how rhetoric is regarded as almost necessary for the effective presentation of philosophy.

The Greek rhetorical theory which was taught in the Roman republic is known from handbooks like the *Rhetoric to Herennius* or Cicero's early work *On Invention*. Cicero's later rhetorical treatises are more philosophical and draw more on the author's experience and Roman conditions, but present substantially the same system of traditional learning. The ideal orator as a man knowledgeable in all subjects is discussed at length in *On the Orator*. *Brutus* deals with the history of oratory, *The Orator* with Cicero's theory of style. Subsequently, the transition at Rome from republic to empire put some rein on political oratory, which became more the expression of predetermined opinion than a form of open debate, but the senate continued to meet and the law courts were mobbed. As if to compensate for its loss of practical influence, rhetoric increased rather than loosened its hold on the educational system. It even became the fashion for adults to engage in the exercises in declamation which had been devised to practice the young.[4] The Romans were highly conservative about all their institutions, and though they observed the tendency toward artificiality in rhetorical education, they did little to check it. Declamation attracted many as an outlet for the fundamental urge to speak and for artistic creativity. It is in this tradition of belief in the importance of rhetorical education and practice that Quintilian's career must be viewed.

### III  *Quintilian's Life*

According to Jerome and the poet Ausonius,[5] both of whom lived in the fourth century A.D., Quintilian came from Calagurris in Spain. There were two places of this name, but the larger was a flourishing town on the Ebro River. It had Roman citizenship and must have been a civilized sort of place: there are remains of a circus and an aqueduct. Although the date of Quintilian's birth is not known, it is clear that he was studying rhetoric in Rome about A.D. 57 and he might reasonably be assumed to have been somewhere between fourteen and twenty at the time. This suggests that he was born a few years before or after A.D. 40, probably not so early as 35 which is often given as the date of his birth. Little is known about Quintilian's father. The fact that a declamation by him is once quoted (IX,iii,73) does not prove he was a rhetorician, but shows that he must have been well educated. The elder Seneca[6] speaks of another rhetorician named Quintilian who could have been our author's grandfather. The family was certainly not a member of the senatorial aristocracy, and thus lacked not only the advantage but also the prejudices which that entailed; it may, however, have been of equestrian rank.

Provincial or Italian boys of good families often had their primary education in their home towns and then, if their parents could afford it, were sent off to study rhetoric in the capital. We may guess that Quintilian's life followed this pattern, and that he came to Rome when about fifteen, but he may have been much younger.[7] If he was born about A.D. 40, this would have brought him to Rome by 56. It was a good time in Roman history, for during the first few years of Nero's reign most public policy was in the hands of Seneca and the praetorian prefect Burrus, and Nero had hardly yet begun to practice the roles in which historians love to cast him.

We can be reasonably certain that Quintilian was in Rome in the year A.D. 57, since he mentions the trial of Capito which took place then.[8] Furthermore, he mentions having heard the orator Servilius Nonianus, who died in A.D. 59, and most important, he knew rather well Domitius Afer, who also died in 59.[9] It had always been the custom in the ancient world for young men with ambitions in public life to fix upon some older model of their ambition, listen to his speeches, talk to him as he walked about town, in some cases even to live with him, and in any event to regard him as a mentor. Cicero had done this with Crassus, Caelius had done it with Cicero, and Quintilian, who praises the practice,[10] apparently did something similar with Afer. He says that he knew Afer "when he was old and I was young" (V,vii,7) and that he not only read his writings, but learned many things from him at first hand. The association lasted long enough for Quintilian to become aware of a change in Afer. He regrets that Afer continued to plead cases when his powers were failing and his audience ridiculed him, for his considered opinion is that "of all the orators whom it has been my lot to know, he was by far the greatest" (XII,xi,3).

Though none of Afer's speeches or writings survive, it is possible to form some impression of the influence he had on Quintilian. Much of it, like the impact of any teacher, was probably general rather than specific. Afer was a real-life orator. Though he doubtless some-times declaimed, his fame came from the law courts. Quintilian also was active in the law courts and was not, like some of his contemporaries, a purely academic orator. Moreover, Afer was distinguished from other orators of the first century by what Quintilian calls the "maturity" of his style (XII,x,11). We are told by Pliny,[11] who had heard it from Quintilian, that Afer spoke gravely and slowly, and Quintilian himself says that he disliked too smooth prose rhythms and broke up any combinations of words which might suggest "tender or delicate voluptuousness." [12] This is not very much information, but suggests that Afer did not cultivate the artificially elaborated style common among orators of the time of Seneca and that he belonged to the more austere and classical tradition which Quintilian himself expounded. We know that Afer encouraged Quintilian's admiration for Virgil (X,i,86), and possibly he inspired his love of Cicero, whose style had been out of favor for some time. A characteristic feature of Afer, which Quintilian repeatedly mentions in Book VI, was his wit, and this is Ciceronian. In contrast, most of the pompous declaimers of imperial Rome took themselves very seriously.

Afer appears also in the pages of the historians Tacitus and Dio Cassius, but in a rather different color from that of Quintilian's beloved master. Tacitus admits his eloquence, but stigmatizes his character: he was perhaps the best example of the *delator*, the professional informer, who worked his way to fame "by any crime" and especially by malicious prosecution which earned him both money and the favor of princes.[13] Afer's first big case was his conviction of Claudia Pulchra in A.D. 26, nominally of "inchastity, adultery, poisoning, and witchcraft," actually probably of conspiracy against the Emperor Tiberius, whose gratitude he openly received. Under Caligula, Afer found himself the object of prosecution, but saved his life and achieved the consulship by abject flattery. Under Claudius he successfully continued his career, even venturing to oppose some of the emperor's freedmen (VI,iii,81).

"Informer" is, of course, a prejorative word for a perfectly legal, if ignoble, profession, and one almost necessary under the Roman system, which lacked a prosecuting attorney. Quintilian knew Afer only late in life when he may have risen above a seedy early reputation, if such he had with his own contemporaries. Tacitus, the enemy of the princes, would see little to admire in an orator who worked harmoniously with any reigning emperor, as Afer had done, however scrupulous the motives or actions of the orator were. Unlike those whom Tacitus admires, Afer supported the principate, and we may even guess that he thought his support was constructive public service. One ironic sentence survives to show his impatience with those who lacked patriotism.[14] Quintilian was to follow in Afer's tradition of service. He did not have Tacitus' attitudes toward the principate. He worked under and received the support of four emperors in turn. He was willing to indulge in a certain amount of courtly language; others might call it flattery. He exercised an influence in favor of humanity and liberality, but he did not tilt against windmills, and he doubtless looked the other way more than was good for his conscience.

Sometime after the death of Afer in 59, Quintilian apparently returned to Spain. Very probably, his education reasonably complete, he went home to practice law in the provincial courts; it was a normal thing to do. Perhaps he went to Calagurris, perhaps to the provincial capital of Terraco, modern Terragona near Barcelona. In any event, he was absent from Rome during the most lurid part of Nero's reign, including the time of the conspiracy of Piso and the fire of Rome.

The next we hear of him, and the most securely dated event of his life, is the report in Jerome's *Chronicle* under the year 68: "M. Fabius Quintilianus is brought to Rome by Galba." Galba was the aged and respectable governor of Hither Spain who was acclaimed emperor in 68 and marched on Rome, where he ruled briefly as Nero's successor until assassinated early in 69. This was the first phase of the period of civil war known as the Year of the Four Emperors. Plutarch[15] suggests that there had been a good deal of litigation in Spain during the previous years as the result of the operations of Nero's agents, which Galba disliked. Possibly Quintilian came to the governor's favorable attention in this connection, but he is never mentioned as one of his close advisers. Suetonius[16] reports that Galba conscripted all the Romans and provincials he could in Spain to augment his forces before setting out, and that he brought along a special group of young men of equestrian rank as a kind of guard. Quintilian may have found himself somewhere in this entourage, but he never mentions Galba.[17] Galba's progress from Spain to Rome was not uneventful, and we may imagine Quintilian's excitement in participating in the great game of king-making.

## IV  *Quintilian's School*

Once arrived in the capital, with Galba soon dead and opportunities for legal practice severely limited by the chaotic conditions of the time,[18] Quintilian apparently decided to open a school of rhetoric. Under A.D. 88, Jerome has the note: "Quintilian, a man of Calagurris in Spain, was the first person to conduct a publicly established school at Rome and receive a salary from the state treasury, and he grew famous." The date 88 is probably an appropriate *floruit*, for Quintilian would have been between forty-five and fifty years old at that time. But if he was the first to receive an appointment, the event must in fact be dated much earlier. According to Suetonius, Vespasian established subsidies of a hundred-thousand sesterces a year for teachers of Latin and Greek rhetoric,[19] and the later historian Zonaras, drawing on a lost portion of Dio Cassius, indicates that this took place in A.D. 71, immediately after Titus' triumphal return from the capture of Jerusalem. Indeed, the announcement was probably part of a new program for a happier world at peace. Vespasian in general was not especially interested in the arts, but he was interested in education as a means of creating an intelligent and responsible ruling class, and Quintilian would have appealed to him.[20] They both had a straightforward honesty and practicality and non-aristocratic backgrounds, and Quintilian's educational and literary ideas were as much a reaction to the period of Nero as was Vespasian's rather homey court.

Before this time, wealthy Romans both in and out of the government had patronized teachers, and there had been tutors at the imperial court, but the regular payment of a public professor out of State funds was a break in tradition. Vespasian probably modeled his subsidy after the foundations to support teachers in Greek cities. We do not know what was expected of Quintilian in return for his salary, but he probably made no charge for his ordinary lectures and criticism. The effect of the subsidy was to free him from minor concerns, to stamp him with approval as a loyal Roman educator, and to make his school famous and prestigious. The salary was doubtless augmented by other income from clients or maybe from some private pupils; in itself it was adequate, but hardly princely, perhaps the equivalent in purchasing power to a good professorial salary in America. Remmius Palaemon, a few years before, had been making four times as much from his private grammar school.[21]

Though he was often busy in the courts, much of Quintilian's time went into the direction of this rhetorical school. Here he gave extensive lectures on rhetorical theory, two courses of which were published by his pupils in an unauthorized edition (I,*pr.*,7). He delivered and discussed declamations. He listened to and criticized the work of his students. Presumably he had assistants, as did other rhetoricians, but he does not say so. His students were mostly boys in their teens from good families; among those who definitely studied with him, the younger Pliny is the most famous.[22] But adults frequently visited the rhetorical schools and sometimes even took part in the exercises, and because of Quintilian's special position, he may have attracted a large crowd of men. Pliny says his older acquaintance, Julius Naso, was often there.

Some of the particular problems which Quintilian faced in teaching will be discussed in a later chapter. He would like his readers to believe that he put more emphasis on moral values than others had, that his school was less out of touch with practical realities of life and oratory in the courts, and this claim may have some validity. What is most clear is that he attempted to cultivate a more classical literary style than had become popular. In the early days of his school, he says (X,i,125–126), the literary idol of the young was Seneca the philosopher, whose staccato epigrams and vivid figures infected the writings of boys with a striving for bizarre effects. Quintilian's aim was to substitute Cicero for Seneca as a touchstone of style, and in this he was partially successful. Ciceronianism in the history of European prose owes some debt to the efforts of Quintilian and others like him in Roman schools.

## V  Quintilian's Legal Practice

During this central period of his career, under Vespasian and Titus and during part of the reign of Domitian, Quintilian was not only teaching, but appeared regularly in the law courts as a patron for clients. Lawyer is not quite the word for this function: like other Roman pleaders he had no special training in law, but turned for technical legal advice if necessary to a jurisconsult. His job was to organize the case and deliver a set speech for plaintiff or defendant, and to examine, or cross-examine, the witnesses.

Quintilian speaks as though he had appeared in many cases, but he only mentions four specifically.[23] The earliest was the case of Naevius of Arpinum, in which the crucial question was whether Naevius had thrown his wife from some height, possibly a window, or whether, as Quintilian argued, she had jumped of her own accord. He clearly won the case, since he published the speech "led by a youthful desire for glory." This was his only authoritatively published speech, though inaccurate versions of some others had been taken down in court and could be bought at bookstalls (VII,ii,24). Their existence shows how famous he must have been. Another successful speech was a testamentary case in which he defended a woman accused of forging her husband's will (IX,ii,73). The matter was a delicate one, since the allegedly forged will was actually an illegal attempt made by the husband himself to create a kind of trust under which his money would be conveyed to his wife. Apparently she could not inherit because of some condition such as that in the *Lex Voconia* which limited the size of estates which could be willed to a wife. If Quintilian treated the case candidly and proved the will by introducing evidence of the bond which the trustees had given, there was danger of having the whole thing declared illegal and thus of losing the inheritance. He claims to have solved this rhetorical challenge by the use of "figures," that is, by veiled language in which the jury came to understand and sympathize with the situation, but no specific statement or evidence which could be used against the wife was advanced.

The third case he mentions must have been most unusual and again suggests that he was very famous at the time. It was a trial involving Berenice of Judaea, sister of King Agrippa II, in a case over which she herself presided and in which Quintilian spoke on her behalf (IV,i,19). Berenice was a kind of latter-day Cleopatra. She had come to know Vespasian's elder son Titus, and in hopes of marriage pursued him to Rome from Palestine in A.D. 75 and again in 79 when he became emperor.[24] Since the second visit was a very brief one, Quintilian's speech is apt to have been delivered in 75. Berenice of course had no right of jurisdiction under Roman law, but she could have tried a member of her own household on almost any charge, and Titus may have arranged for Quintilian to appear. Possibly she was amused by legal procedures: it is recorded that she attended the trial of Paul.[25] The fourth case is the least known, but centered around the allegation that a young girl was a sister of Quintilian's client (VI,i,39). Probably it was a testamentary case, and probably Quintilian won; at least he was able to thwart the melodramatic appeal of the girl to her alleged brother by hustling his client out of court in time.

We can form some judgment of Quintilian as an orator from his discussion of rhetorical problems, from a few examples he gives of the way to treat declamations, and from his style in arguing for or against various rhetorical doctrines. For example, he describes (VI,ii,29) his method of becoming emotionally involved in a case by reliving in his mind, and probably also vividly describing, the various details. It was perhaps this that made him so effective in opening a case. He says (IV,ii,86) that when he cooperated with other patrons he usually handled the statement of the case, thus leaving at least the peroration, and perhaps the argumentation, to others.

## VI    De Causis

About the year 89 Quintilian wrote a treatise *De Causis Corruptae Eloquentiae (On the Causes of Corrupted Eloquence)*.[26] This work is usually, though wrongly, thought of as similar to other discussions of literary decline which were common in the first century A.D.: the prefaces to the work of the elder Seneca, the literary digression of the historian Velleius Paterculus, the opening passages of the extant portion of Petronius' novel, the end of the Greek treatise *On Sublimity*, attributed to Longinus, and Tacitus' *Dialogue on Orators*.

Belief in a general pattern of cultural decline, rather than in the progress usually assumed in the modern world, was deeply fixed in the ancient mind and was especially congenial to the Romans, who were always inclined to think that all change was change for the worse. In the early empire it seems to have been quite widely thought that literature, of which the prime prose form was oratory, was decaying. This belief had some validity, but it ought not to be accepted at face value. The situation had many aspects. The empire had obviated the factional disputes of the late republic and by so doing had reduced the need for political oratory, in many ways a happy result. But what speaking there was in the senate or on ceremonial occasions often became routine, or worse, lacking in independence. Moreover, though the emperors occasionally claimed to welcome freedom of speech, they hardly lived up to their word. Opposition was so choked that when it did break out it was violent and irresponsible, and this tended to make the emperors suspicious of all criticism. The law courts were busier than ever, but the opportunities there for great oratory seemed more limited, partly because of changes in procedure, and cases almost never took on the national significance that the factionalism of the late republic had encouraged. Declamation flourished as never before, but it was an artificial art form with little substance and much emphasis on verbal cleverness. The obsession with preserving the status quo, so badly shaken in the first century B.C., helped to strengthen the ordinary traditionalism and made it seem as though nothing new had been or could be said in any literary form. There were indeed able orators and poets, but there was no Cicero and no Virgil. Perhaps belief in decline was exaggerated for the very reason that the age was an elegant and cultured one which put a premium on literary composition. Their own inadequacy rankled writers of the empire.

The elder Seneca, writing under Tiberius, suggested three possible reasons for decline.[27] The first, which he inclined to favor, was that it resulted from moral degeneration due to luxury. People had been made lazy; they had less ambition. The second possibility was the lack of incentive under the empire, which might be extended to its negative side, the fear of repression. And third was fate, which might be more elaborately stated as some kind of cyclical view of literary history. The other authors fit into one or more of these categories of explanation, except for Petronius.[28] He is apparently satirizing speeches on the causes of decline rather than writing a serious essay, but the major point is the bad influence of the educational system, especially the vogue for bizarre and bombastic declamation.

The title of Quintilian's lost treatise is often loosely translated *On the Causes of the Decline of Eloquence,* as though Quintilian, like the authors just discussed, was seeking to explain a general decline. But there is little reason to believe that Quintilian concerned himself with a general literary decline. He discussed the nature and popularity of certain kinds of style of which he disapproved; he is not likely to have stressed the literary inferiority of the age of Domitian to other periods. Domitian had made panegyric orations on Jupiter a regular part of the new Capitoline games in A.D. 86, and it is even possible that Quintilian's work was part of an unofficial program to encourage literature. In the *Institutio,* Quintilian never shows any concern with the effect of political conditions on eloquence. He approves of the empire as a constitution which has removed many of the dangers to which a republic is subject and substituted the care and protection of the prince (VI,i,35). He claims in one passage that no age is happier than his own, since it can profit from the accumulated examples of the past (XII,xi,22); he rejects any natural decline (XII,xi,25); he thinks highly of many writers of his own time (II,v,23–24; X,i,122), and in reviewing Latin literature in Book X gives no hint of any general inferiority of the first century A.D. to the first century B.C. Yet he is highly moral and strongly disapproves of many features of contemporary society, vividly pointing out, for example, that children were in as great danger of corruption at home as in school (I,ii,6–8). He clearly did believe that vitiated tastes and mistaken literary fashions exercised a pernicious effect on certain writers and that education in some ways had lost standards and sensibility.

In the *Institutio*, Quintilian criticizes those who think that the corrupted style is especially popular or persuasive, and he lists seven aspects of corruption: license in the choice of words, childish epigrams, unrestrained pomposity, empty commonplaces, fragile adornments, extravagance mistaken for sublimity, and madness mistaken for freedom of speech (XII,x,73). People have come to believe that natural speech lacks ability, and they prefer the contorted as something exquisite (II,v,11). He claims (VIII,iii,58) to have discussed, presumably in *De Causis*, the fact that speech is corrupted in the same number of ways in which it is adorned, a view which could easily be applied to the seven aspects of corruption listed. We know specifically that *De Causis* contained a discussion of the limits and uses of hyperbole (VIII,vi,76), a virtue which easily becomes a fault. Apparently the history of declamation was reviewed (II,iv,42). In the *Institutio* (II,x,3), Quintilian claims that through the fault of teachers, the license and ignorance of declaimers have become leading corrupters of eloquence. Probably in the earlier work he criticized teachers for tolerating artificiality and not making declamation an exercise in argumentation (V,xii,23). In sum, the loss of *De Causis Corruptae Eloquentiae* is perhaps not a great one since the work may be viewed as a preliminary exposition of some of the views later set forth in the *Institutio*.

## VII  *Quintilian's Retirement*

After twenty years of teaching, Quintilian retired (I,*pr.*,1). He says he gave up his career as a pleader at the same time (II,xii,12). He may mean the twenty years as a round number; he may mean twenty years in his position as a state paid teacher. The exact date is thus difficult to determine, but a date of around A.D. 90 fits into the rest of the chronology of his life. If that is correct, he was about fifty. Why did he retire? There are many good reasons for retirement, and the chief difficulty is knowing which ones carried the greatest weight with Quintilian. At the very beginning of the *Institutio*, he speaks of the leisure he had at last obtained. Desire for leisure might be more frankly expressed as desire to be a gentleman. Conducting a rhetorical school had certainly become more respectable with the years, but earning money was always lacking in gentility at Rome. Juvenal [29] cites Quintilian as an apparently unique example of a

teacher who became wealthy, and Quintilian himself may have felt
that once he was economically secure he should retire. His fellow
Spaniard Martial [30] addressed a little poem to him which is interesting in this connection:

> Quintilian, greatest director of straying youth,
>     You are an honor, Quintilian, to the Roma toga.
> Because though poor I make haste to enjoy life before
>     worn out by years,
>     Forgive me. No one is quick enough at living.
> A man who longs to surpass his father's census rating
>     And crowds his hall with showy busts
> May put off his pleasure if he will.
> A hearth and a roof stained with black smoke
>     And a running spring and an untrimmed yard
> Please me. Let me have a plump home-born slave,
>     An unlearned wife, a good night's sleep, a day
>     without a lawsuit.

The poem was published in 86 and may have been written a year
or two earlier. It is a traditional expression of love for the simple
life reminiscent of Horace,[31] and it may have a slight element of sour
grapes in it, but there is no reason why it is not applicable throughout
to Quintilian as Martial saw him. The opening tribute, which is all
that is usually quoted, seems sincere: Quintilian is honored, in the
first line, as a teacher and in the second as an orator. There is a clear
hint, however, that he is driven by ambition for wealth and position,
and the last line seems to imply that his life involves some strain.
The unlearned wife Martial prefers may be a contrast too. Quintilian
thought women should be educated (I,i,6), and it is only too likely
that he had taken in hand his young wife. What Martial thought he
saw, others may have noted, and Quintilian himself may have felt it
and been eager for retirement.

The second reason Quintilian gives was a desire to retire "while
I would still be missed" (II,xii,12). Readers have always thought of
Domitius Afer, who continued to speak when his powers were declining, and have concluded that Quintilian was anxious to avoid this.
It is also possible that he had grown slightly weary of his school;
the chapters on education give the impression of a fading interest
in educational reform.

Finally, there is the possibility suggested by the date of A.D. 90
or thereabouts to anyone familiar with Roman history. Domitian was

at best a difficult man to please, gloomy and solitary, but ambitious, demanding, legalistic, and puritanical. At the beginning of A.D. 89, he had an experience from which he never totally recovered: a dangerous revolt by Saturninus, who was in command of the army in Germany. The revolt was put down, but it aroused in the emperor feelings of suspicion and insecurity which lasted until his assassination in 96. Domitian regarded the senate as his natural enemy, and the senators returned the compliment. Although the number executed was not great, most of those who escaped, Tacitus and Pliny among them, never forgot the experience, and never forgave Domitian. The emperor apparently made constant use of unscrupulous orators and informers in his police state methods. Quintilian was probably not in much personal danger so long as he remained discreet, but his friends and pupils included those most opposed to the emperor, and he can hardly be blamed for not wanting to do the emperor's dirty work as a pleader or to be officially connected with the regime as a teacher. He had served under the Flavians and supported them, including Domitian, but there were limits. A.D. 90 was an excellent time to retire.

## VIII  *Composition and Publication of the* Institutio

According to the preface to the first book, after his retirement Quintilian was urged by friends to write a treatise on the art of speaking. It is difficult to know how seriously to take this request, for it is a convention among Roman writers that their works are produced in response to friendly demands, but such requests were sometimes certainly made.[32] Quintilian was, after all, an authority on a subject of great contemporary interest and had made himself the spokesman for a particular view of education and rhetoric, so that it is not strange if his friends and former pupils welcomed a statement of his views.

The only one of these friends identified by name is Marcellus Vitorius, to whom the finished work is dedicated.[33] Quintilian describes him as a good friend and a lover of literature, and he hopes the work will be helpful in the education of his son, Geta. Marcellus held high office in Rome, capping his career with the consulship in A.D. 105. His literary interests are borne out by the fact that the poet Statius dedicated to him the fourth book of the *Silvae*, and it is possible that he is also the Marcellus to whom the grammarian Valerius Probus dedicated a literary epistle.[34]

A close literary circle around Marcellus is too much to deduce from the evidence, but it seems probable that Quintilian knew both Statius and Probus, as well as Martial and Pliny. He never mentions any of them, but it is not his custom to mention living authors. Probus collected manuscripts, corrected and punctuated them, and wrote textual and grammatical commentaries. He published little and did not teach a school, but he sometimes discussed his work with a few friends. After an initial disappointment in his career, he seems to have lived a retired, bookish life. Suetonius is our main source about him and says that his literary tastes were restricted to authors much out of fashion.[35] What he appears to have liked were the classical Latin poets: Terence, Lucretius, Virgil, Horace, and from the empire, Persius. Not Ovid, or Lucan, or Seneca. Quintilian would have had some sympathy with this critical position.

The case of Statius is more complicated, and it is doubtful that he and Quintilian were on the best of terms. Statius was a facile poet and in considerable demand for recitation. He claimed to be a humble follower of Virgil [36] and certainly imitated him, but he also wrote an exaggerated tribute to Lucan,[37] and his poetry has many of the flaws, especially the uncontrolled hyperbole, to which Quintilian objected. Statius was an assiduous flatterer of Domitian or anyone else, but not always successfully. He lost the Capitoline contest, and he may well have envied Quintilian's secure position. In the dedication to Marcellus Vitorius of the fourth book of the *Silvae*, a series of occasional poems, Statius says that he has included in the book more than the usual number of poems to show that he is unmoved by those who, so he hears, criticize them as trivial. Whoever does not like them does not have to read them. Now it is possible that he has Quintilian in mind, for Quintilian expresses disapproval of a *silva* (X,iii,17), which he defines as a hasty composition written on the impulse of the moment and then unsuccessfully polished. The passage is not very pointedly directed at Statius' poems, since Quintilian is talking about quick rough composition in prose or verse and uses the word *silva* in the singular rather than in the plural, but it is very possible that he was heard to say that Statius' poems were an example of what he disliked.

The fourth book of the *Silvae* was definitely published in A.D. 95, and the passage just discussed suggests that the *Institutio* was already out. The question of the date of composition and publication of the *Institutio* is difficult. Quintilian refers to his retirement as sometime before. He says in the introductory letter to his bookseller, Trypho, that he spent "a little more than two years" writing the work, mostly on the research. Doubtless he means an elapsed time of two years during which writing was interspersed with research. Because of the complimentary references to Domitian, there is no doubt that it was published before that emperor's assassination in September of 96.

Probably the best evidence of date is the statement in the discussion of epic poetry, "we recently lost much in Valerius Flaccus" (X,i,90). This Valerius is the author of the extant *Argonautica*. Now the *Argonautica* contains references to the Sarmatians, which probably refer to military events of A.D. 89 or possibly 92, and in the introduction it contains what seems to be a clear reference to the temple of the Flavian *gens*.[38] Martial [39] celebrates the completion of this temple in a poem in Book IX published in 94 and probably written that year, since he was publishing roughly a book a year of somewhat topical verse, and would have included it in Book VIII if it had been written in time. Valerius Flaccus' reference, unlike Martial's, does not have to be to the completed temple, but it can hardly have been written more than a year or so earlier, and it is thus evidence that Valerius did not die before A.D. 93. If we assume that Quintilian retired in 90, we could then allow a year or so before he was induced to begin work on the *Institutio*. He would then have begun work perhaps in 92. As we shall see, he seems to have written in roughly the order in which the books stand. This would put Book X fairly late in 93 or early 94, and completion and publication perhaps in 94, certainly by 95.

Some confirmation for this hypothesis may be derived from the honor that came to Quintilian through the efforts of Flavius Clemens, who obtained for him the *ornamenta consularia*,[40] the rights of dress and precedence of one who had been consul, but without any of the duties of a senator. Flavius Clemens was a first cousin of Domitian and was married to Domitilla, the daughter of the emperor's sister. He was consul during the first half of A.D. 95, but disgraced and executed before the year was out on a charge of atheism or Jewish practices, which has been taken to mean Christianity.[41] It is unlikely that he secured consular honors for another before his own consulship, or at least before he was consul elect,[42] and an occasion for honor would have been the recent publication of Quintilian's great work, a public service.

Quintilian's original plan was probably to write the *Institutio* completely as a private person, with no dedication or address to any member of the imperial household. When he was about one-quarter of the way through, however, he was suddenly put in charge of the education of two sons of Flavius Clemens, whom Domitian had marked out for his heirs and renamed Vespasian and Domitian (IV, *pr.*,2; VI,*pr.*,1). This trust was clearly not sought and may well have been against Quintilian's wishes, but it could not very well be refused. Suetonius[43] says the boys were little (*parvulos*), but what that means is impossible to say. There is a coin of Smyrna inscribed, in Greek, "Vespasian the younger," with the portrait of a young man, not a child.[44] The date is not known nor is it absolutely certain that Quintilian's pupil is meant, though it seems likely. Quintilian himself does not mention the age of his pupils, but he seems to have expected to teach them rhetoric, and we may guess that the older one at least was in his teens. It would be interesting to know what happened to the boys. If they had been alive when Domitian died, it seems likely that they would have been considered as possible heirs, but the sources say nothing at all, neither that they were considered nor that they were disposed of in some way. They may, of course, have died from natural causes at any time. If they met with foul play, a possible occasion, other than the time of Domitian's own death, would be the death of their natural father in 95. If this is true, it is confirmation of the publication of the *Institutio* before the fall of Flavius Clemens, since reference to them could easily have been removed from the text before publication.

What little more is known about Quintilian is derived from the preface to the sixth book of the *Institutio,* in which he describes the successive deaths of his wife and his two sons. This celebrated passage is not typical of Quintilian's manner, for he is nowhere else so personal or so emotional, nor is it very well written: the attitude toward the gods or fate is not clear and, though there is dignity in the despair at the end, the philosophical statements are commonplace; the curses on literary composition because of the coincident loss of his sons contrast strangely with the subsequent acceptance of literary composition as a solace; the praise of his sons becomes slightly gauche; sentences are too long and too rambling. But the passage is an important one and much can be discovered from reading it carefully. Most evident is the complete acceptance of the system and practice of rhetoric as a good in itself. Quintilian liked children and he obviously loved his sons. The natural way for him to express his love is built up out of figures of speech and techniques of rhetorical amplification. The lack of philosophical coherence is characteristic of Quintilian, so is the determination to make the best of the situation. There is also a hint of the ambition which Martial remarked, though it need not be held against him; he had arranged for his only surviving son to be adopted by a family of consular rank and he had, before the boy was ten, arranged his marriage with the daughter of a praetor who was Quintilian's brother-in-law.[45] If the older boy was about ten when he died, and this was around A.D. 93, he was born in 83. Since both sons were born before Quintilian's wife was nineteen years old, it seems likely that they were married about 82 and that she was seventeen. She was clearly a lady of good family. He would have been in his early forties.

Nothing is kown about the end of Quintilian's life. The references to him in Pliny seem to suggest that he was no longer alive in the first decade of the second century, and it is likely that he died about the same time as Domitian, A.D. 96, but we may not assume any connection between the two deaths, for no source remarks on what would have been most worthy of remark. A letter of Pliny's[46] addressed to some Quintilian whose daughter is about to be married may be to a brother or cousin of the rhetorician or simply to someone who happens to have had the same name; otherwise we must assume that Quintilian lived on to marry again and have a daughter, all of which seems improbable.

Quintilian had the questionable pleasure of living through an "interesting" period in human history. During his lifetime the empire was expanding in Britain and elsewhere, almost to its limits. The Christian religion was ominously spreading to Rome and beyond. Pompeii and Herculaneum were engulfed in the most famous volcanic eruption of all time. The Colosseum was building in Rome. And the empire was split in one of its intermittent wars of succession. Over his life and all his experience towered the nearly divine figures of the art-crazed Nero, the blunt Vespasian, the affable Titus, and the menacing Domitian. He seems not to have survived to see the "rare felicity" of the times of the five good emperors.

# CHAPTER 2

## *On the Education of the Orator*

QUINTILIAN perhaps intended that his great work should be known as *De Institutione Oratoria (On the Education of the Orator)*. That is what he calls it in the prefaced letter to the bookseller Trypho.[1] The word *institutio* had been used by Cicero and Seneca of systematic training or education of the intellect. It implies the implantation of knowledge in the mind. There was a Latin word *educatio* which had been used in a general way by earlier authors, but Quintilian seems to have felt this was more properly limited to physical or moral nurture.[2]

The division of the work into twelve books is Quintilian's own, as references in the text indicate,[3] and many of the subdivisions of the books represent such clear breaks in the subject matter that some kind of organization into chapters must have been in Quintilian's mind: the various chapters of Book VI are a particularly clear example. But some chapters are illogical units, and the numbers and titles are very likely the work of some later scribe; Quintilian never refers to them. The scribe marked off *prooemia*, or introductions, to seven of the books, but as far as the subject matter goes he might as well have designated the *prooemia* of Books V and VII as chapters or have made the first seven sections of the first chapter of Book III into a separate *prooemium*. The introductions to Books IV and VI are the personal ones, occasioned respectively by Quintilian's appointment as tutor to Domitian's heirs and by the death of his elder son. The remaining introductions mark out the major divisions of the work and indicate Quintilian's plan and objective. Roughly speaking, that to the first book introduces the work as a whole, that to Book VIII serves as a transition from the group of books dealing with invention to the group dealing with style, that to Book XII points out the problems and originality of the unique last book.

## I  *The* Prooemium *of Book I*

The introduction to the first book is naturally of special interest. It falls into three parts. The first (I,*pr.*,1–8) explains why Quintilian writes: after his retirement, friends had asked him to write something on the art of speaking. He had objected that there were many such works. The friends replied, however, that there was much disagreement among writers on rhetoric, and even if Quintilian could not say anything original, he ought to offer a judgment among conflicting views.

This objective is discussed again at the beginning of Book III, and is in fact a persistent feature of the *Institutio*. In arriving at a definition of rhetoric, for example, Quintilian reviews a large number of earlier definitions, gives his criticism of them, and finally settles on "the science of speaking well," which is substantially the definition of the Stoic philosophers Chrysippus and Cleanthes (II,xv,33–38). More often, he felt, it was not necessary to offer such an extensive historical survey, but to counteract the teaching of Celsus, or the style of Seneca, or to choose between two schools of thought, for example between the views of the Apollodoreans and the Theodoreans.[4] Quintilian himself certainly did not belong to either of these two pedantic schools which split rhetorical hairs in the early empire (III,i,18). He claims that he belongs to no sect at all (IV, i,22); that though he has brought together a variety of opinion, final choice must be with the reader (IX,iv,2); and that he will sometimes be original, but when that is not possible he will be content to be thought careful (III,i,22).

The *Institutio* is not, however, solely a survey and judgment of earlier rhetoric. In the *prooemium* to Book I Quintilian goes on to say that once he had begun he could not be content with so modest an aim. He must pay back the confidence of his friends; he must do more than tread in the footsteps of others. This desire to make the most constructive possible use of a situation or opportunity is characteristic of him as both a person and a scholar. It is what made it possible for him to work for Domitian and to keep on going after the death of his sons. More fundamentally, it was perhaps this trait of character which drew him to rhetoric, once defined by Aristotle as the faculty of discovering, on every subject, the possible means of persuasion: what can be done, what can be said, what graces of style can be employed. The rhetorician must be fascinated with a challenge. The opportunity which Quintilian saw in the work he had agreed to write was to take a much broader view and study the training of the orator throughout his whole life, beginning with infancy. "Almost all" who have written on the art of pleading have ignored elementary education, he claims (I,*pr.*,4), either out of contempt for the insignificance of primary studies, or because it is the business of the grammarian, not the rhetorician, or because the subject is not a very showy one, "as the gables of a building are seen, but the foundation is hid." In the past, individuals had sometimes taught both grammar and rhetoric, but in Quintilian's time there was apparently a kind of uneasiness between the two professions. He says at the beginning of Book II that rhetoricians had lost interest in everything but declamation and that grammarians had taken to teaching what were once preliminary rhetorical exercises. Quintilian never gives us reason to conclude that he had taught in a grammar school himself, though he is certainly familiar with the subject. He will not refuse to begin his account of an orator's education from the time the potential orator is still *infans*—unable to speak.

The words "almost all" suggest that Quintilian's scope had some precedent, though no other work has survived with the coverage of the *Institutio*. In a letter describing the writings of Pliny the Elder, the younger Pliny[5] mentions an extensive work called *The Student* "which formed and perfected the orator from the cradle." It was apparently the elder Pliny's only work on rhetoric. Quintilian lists Pliny among recent writers on rhetoric and describes his work as pedantic (XI,iii,143). In another passage, without naming Pliny, he contrasts the practical orator at whom he aims with the "student" of declamation (II,x,15). But though Pliny's treatment may not much have appealed to Quintilian, the scope of his work did constitute a kind of precedent.[6]

Quintilian's explanation of why he writes concludes with some miscellaneous reasons: the work will be a pledge of his friendship for Marcellus Vitorius and may be helpful in the education of the latter's son Geta. Finally, it will replace two accounts of the art of rhetoric which had been published without his authorization, based on lectures which he had given, one a short course for beginners, the other more extensive and intended for older students. This passage makes clear what was in fact to be expected, that Quintilian's lectures to his school were the basis of the discussion of rhetoric in the *Institutio*: "some things will be the same, many changed, more added, all will be more carefully arranged and worked out as much as I can" (I,*pr.*,8).

Up to this point the implication is that Quintilian plans to enlarge the scope of his discussion only by beginning with an account of pre-rhetorical studies. In fact, his plan is also to give an account of rhetoric fuller than found in many authors and to add a discussion of the adult orator. The next section of the introduction (I,*pr*.,9–20) begins to prepare us for this enlarged plan. It might be described as dealing with the relationship between rhetoric and philosophy. Quintilian says that he seeks to train the perfect orator. In other words, like Plato at the end of the *Phaedrus* or Cicero in the *Orator,* he sets forth an ideal which has been approached, though never achieved. Later in the work he makes it clear that Cicero and to a lesser extent Demosthenes have come closest. This idealism was an opimistic feature of Quintilian's teaching and in contrast to the view of many of his contemporaries that eloquence was declining. Quintilian then enunciates for the first time his favorite paradox, that no one can be a perfect orator who is not also a good man. The view is Stoic, as is Quintilian's later definition of rhetoric. Possibly it was derived from the philosopher Posidonius, though the view is implied in some of the writings of Plato and is reminiscent of Cato the Elder's definition of an orator as "a good man, skilled in speaking." [7] Yet this does not mean, he is quick to explain, turning the orator into a philosopher. The orator is something far more active, far superior to the philosopher, "a citizen, qualified for the administration of public and private affairs, who can direct cities by his counsels, secure them with laws, and correct them by judicial decisions" (I,*pr*.,10). There are things to be learned from the books of philosophers, and orators will regularly discuss philosophical questions like justice, fortitude, and temperance, but the orator must have something in addition to this, a power of mind and a facility for speaking. Cicero was right, Quintilian says, in claiming that the functions of eloquence and wisdom were once united in the same persons, which is what nature had planned. No concept is more dear to Quintilian than nature. Then a split took place; Cicero[8] blamed it on Socrates, but Quintilian does not mention Socrates and perhaps thought of it as occurring somewhat after his time: orators turned to the pursuit of profit and left morality deserted. Others, without any respect for eloquence, rushed in as teachers and moral philosophers, arrogantly monopolizing the name "students of wisdom." The older philosophers gave good advice and lived as they had advised. At the present time, however, men no longer strive by virtue or study to be considered philosophers. It is a matter of look, squalor, and non-conformity, which cover up the worst possible morals. In this judgment Quintilian reflects the opinion of the Flavian emperors, who had grown weary of the carping of Cynics and some Stoics, and had even expelled them from Rome.[9] Quintilian's criticism of philosophers is hardly a matter of toadying to the emperor, however. His own feeling that it was important always to be positive and constructive made the philosophers seem unattractive.

Quintilian says that what is called philosophy is common to all men. Everyone, unless he is totally worthless, speaks about justice, equity, and right. Even peasants are interested in natural causes. Everyone ought to be concerned about proper and correct speech, but these things are most important to the orator. If he is to be perfect, he must demand back his own from the philosophers. He must be perfect not only in knowledge, but also in wisdom and in the whole art of speaking. Quintilian usually thinks of philosophy as primarily a moral code involved with action, rather than, as Cicero had viewed it, an intellectual study, valuable for the orator. The difference reflects both the personality of the two men and the general decline of abstract philosophy from Hellenistic to imperial times. The second part of the introduction concludes with a few words on the attainability of the ideal orator. Perhaps none has reached it, but the higher we aim the further we will get. There is certainly such a thing as consummate eloquence, and it is not debarred us by nature.

The third part of the introduction (I,*pr.*,21–27) deals more concretely with the structure and substance of the work. The first book will discuss pre-rhetorical studies. The second will examine the first studies with the rhetorician and the nature of rhetoric. Then will come five books (that is, Books III through VII) devoted to invention, to which arrangement is subjoined, then four on *elocutio*, which generally means style, but here involves style, memory, and delivery.

One more book will be added in which we must fashion the orator himself; where we shall describe, in so far as our poor powers allow, what his moral standards ought to be, what his rationale in undertaking, in studying, in speaking cases, what his style of eloquence, what his retirement date, what his interests after retirement. (I,*pr.*,22)

This roughly describes the structure of the work, though Book VII on arrangement is not so clearly set off from Book VI as might be expected, the unusual tenth book is passed over without special mention, and Book XII contains a few topics on the orator's "instruments" which are not here anticipated. The existence of the latter is first suggested at the end of Book II, and they may constitute a kind of afterthought.

The order which Quintilian follows is doubtless obvious, but highly significant. It is the order of nature, of biological development and of oratorical creation. In Book I a child first learns to speak and then to read and write. As he grows, he studies first with the grammarian, progressing through his series of graded exercises, then with the rhetorician. The question of a suitable age for beginning rhetorical studies is examined, as is, later, the right age for first appearing in court and the right age for retirement. After the child reaches the rhetorician, Quintilian turns to the substance of rhetorical theory, with which he is occupied from the middle of Book II to the end of Book XI. In this he follows the order, traditional since Hellenistic times, of invention, arrangement, style, memory, and delivery, an order which recapitulates the work of the orator: he must plan his argumentation, then how to arrange it, how to adorn it, how to prepare for delivery, and what voice and gesture to use in presentation. Once he has presented the orator with all of this necessary rhetorical knowledge, Quintilian can resume his picture of the orator's career in Book XII, looking into moral and intellectual requirements other than rhetoric, the sort of cases the orator will take, the preparations he will make, the styles he will employ, and finally the activities suitable to retirement.

The introduction is addressed to Marcellus Vitorius, but naturally Quintilian expects a wider audience. Not only young Geta, but Domitian's heirs and Quintilian's own son are to be beneficiaries of the work. The first chapter of the first book is apparently addressed to parents. One of the most striking passages is that where Quintilian imagines himself in the character of Aristotle, taking Alexander the Great on his knee to teach him his letters, though every man will think his own son equally precious (I,i,24). Subsequently, however, Quintilian writes for teachers. He is not teaching grammar in Book I, but advising those who are going to teach it (I,iv,17). He often gives advice on teaching methods, as in the introduction to Book VIII where he explains that the teacher must make a choice out of the rules given: the pupil should believe at first that what he has learned is the only way and then discover afterward that it is the best. Occasionally, even in the early part of the work, Quintilian seems to be speaking directly to students. His precepts, he says (II, xii,12; III,vi,64), will be useful to young men of ability. Like Lucretius he has tried to put honey around the cup of his instruction to make it sweeter to the young (III,i,4). In the books on rhetorical theory Quintilian gives advice directly on matters to be used in speaking, and Books X and XII are largely directed to the adult orator himself. There is thus a general change of addressee with the biological growth of the orator.

In Book II,xiv,5 Quintilian points out another structural pattern which may be seen in his work: he will speak of art, of the artist, and of the work of art. The art includes everything in Books III through XI; the artist is discussed in the first nine chapters of Book XII; the work of art is the subject of chapter X of Book XII. Thus these topics are very unequally treated. Quintilian seems to have borrowed them from writers on poetics.[10] Although they perhaps afforded him some kind of precedent in his nervousness at dealing with his subject in a way more comprehensive than other rhetoricians had, they are not really very helpful and the chapter on the work of art seems rather out of place in its present context.

There is some reason to believe that Quintilian not only planned the work along these natural lines, but actually wrote it systematically in pretty much this order, a procedure he himself recommends (III,ix,8–9). At least the prefaces to Books IV, VI, VIII, and XII seem to mark stages in the composition, and the initial omission of an invocation of the emperor is repaired at the beginning of Book IV. He speaks also of the increasing difficulty of his task (VIII,*pr.*,13; XII,*pr.*,1). Book XII has been regarded as showing signs of haste.[11] If so, it confirms Quintilian's claim in the prefatory letter to his bookseller that he was pushed to publish the work before he had planned. The phraseology of that letter *(libros—iam emittere inciperem)* also suggests that the work was published in separate books or groups of books, but Quintilian had certainly completed a draft of the whole before publishing any part. In the *prooemium* to Book I he uses the present tense, as well as the future, of the contents and in one passage even says "whatever we thought useful for educating the orator we have brought together in these twelve books" (I,*pr.*,25). Possibly the introduction was written after Quintilian had completed a first draft of the work, but before he made the final hasty revisions for the publisher. This would explain why the sections added to the last book are not anticipated in the summary of the work just examined. Throughout there are numerous cross references both to what has been said and to what will be discussed. The fact that he had his lectures as a basis for the discussion helped to make this easier to do, but clearly he did check over the cross references before publication.[12]

After outlining the contents of his work, Quintilian makes some other general remarks about it. It will be his aim not only to instruct students in the science which some regard as the whole of rhetoric—he has perhaps the pedantic Pliny in mind, but probably also numerous other technical handbooks—but he will try to nourish eloquence and cover the bare bones with flesh. The best example of this is the famous first chapter of the tenth book where the orator's style is enriched from a study of the monuments of Greek and Roman literature.

The introduction concludes with the proviso that a would-be orator must have some natural gift to start with. Moderate gifts can be improved by study and practice. The triad of nature, study, and practice appears in some form in practically every ancient rhetorician, beginning with the Greek sophists[13] and extending as far afield as the writers of Sanskrit treatises on poetic style. Its presence here is not simply tradition: Quintilian was not one to try to work against nature.

CHAPTER 3

## Quintilian on Education

SCHOOLING was not native to Rome.[1] Tradition required children to be educated at home, first by the mother or nurse. Schools were introduced from Greece, certainly by the third century B.C., but were long viewed with suspicion, and those who could hired private teachers or bought educated slaves. Even in Quintilian's time there was not the view of education as a community responsibility which the Greek states had felt. The family remained the dominant institution in Roman law and custom.

The schools which were opened copied Greek curricula and methods. At the age of about seven boys and girls were sent to a primary school where they were taught to read, write, and count, but little more. Most freeborn children in Rome presumably had at least this much primary education. What we hear about such schools is not very reassuring: they were operated by anybody who pleased in small shops around the city; families paid the teacher directly, but he often made very little; his educational method was rote memorization, and his discipline imposed by the rod.

The second level of education was the grammar school, taught by the *grammaticus*, or grammarian. This took somewhat greater knowledge, and in the late republic and early empire there were even a few distinguished scholars like Remmius Palaemon teaching grammar, but the average social and economic level of the profession remained low, and pictures of grammar schools are also not generally flattering. Roman culture was bilingual and there thus existed both Greek and Latin grammar schools. Quintilian (I,i,14) thinks the two should complement each other. The ordinary grammarian taught the science of speaking correctly and the reading of the poets. That is, he taught grammar in the modern sense and the parsing of works of literature, as well as composition. From discussion of poems, students learned a good deal of mythology, some history, a little music

and astronomy. There perhaps were independent teachers of mathe-
matics, geometry, and other subjects, but it was a rare parent who
had his children exposed to anything but the basic grammatical
curriculum. Greek schools had had a slightly broader curriculum.

Grammar school students included both boys and girls, ranging in
age from nine or ten up to fourteen or fifteen, though older people
sometimes came to the lectures of some famous grammarians. We
have no way of telling what percentage of the population reached
this level, but there were more than twenty large grammar schools
in Rome in the early part of the first century B.C.[2] and probably more
later. Certainly a significant percentage of the Roman citizen population had a grammar school education.

The third level of education was the school of the rhetorician, open
only to boys. Often they were around fourteen when they began, and
they might continue to study rhetoric practically full-time for several
years. This is the kind of school which Quintilian operated for twenty
years. Boys of senatorial and equestrian class ordinarily got this far
in their schooling, and were then regarded as prepared for the great
business of life, which was being a citizen and patron and managing
one's own property. Some might also study law or philosophy, either
in Rome or abroad. Medicine was regarded as menial and usually
left to Greeks or pursued as a kind of hobby; architecture was an
offshoot of military engineering or a Greek trade or, again, a hobby.

Though he accepts this general educational structure, Quintilian
has a number of suggestions to make to parents and teachers. His
influence was on the side of making it more humane, more moral,
more practical, somewhat more profound, slightly broader. Radical
reform of any sort was foreign to the Roman mind, however impera-
tive it sometimes seems to a modern student of Roman affairs. It
almost always failed when imposed. But occasionally public or official awareness could be brought to a problem and some gradual
amelioration hoped for. This is especially true in the first two centuries of the empire, when fire and police protection were begun,
some attempts at slum control and city planning pressed, some provision made for orphans, and private philanthropy indulged. Since
education was widely criticized, especially the impracticality of rhetorical declamation, Quintilian's impulses to reform were characteristic of his age, but the highly conservative nature of the reforms
he suggested were characteristic of his country. It never occurred to
him that broad universal public education was either desirable or
possible.[3] He has nothing to say about the training of slaves or tech-

nicians or about any but the traditional grammatical-rhetorical education. But as regrettable as it is that the Romans overlooked the need to raise the general educational level of society, that is only half of education's goal. The other is the full development of the potential of an able individual. Of this need Quintilian is highly conscious. It is partly what he means by the perfect orator. Quantity does not concern him; quality does. Although he is not especially snobbish or bigoted, he expects this quality orator to come from the upper levels of society. The expenses of education can thus be ignored; it is assumed that a private tutor or admission to a school is equally possible, so that the decision can be made solely on educational grounds, and the child can learn his letters from ivory alphabet blocks, and so on.

In the introduction to his first book Quintilian promises that he will try to judge between conflicting rhetorical theories. This is true also of his remarks on education. The problems which he recognizes had mostly been discussed before. In facing them, he takes the line which seems to him most suitable and gives his reasons, but follows no one authority. He mentions the educational theories of the Stoic philosopher Chrysippus, and he had read Diogenes of Babylon and apparently others who wrote on education, but he makes no reference to the idealized educational proposals of thinkers like Plato. Although he had not himself taught elementary or grammar school, he had closely observed what was taught there in the way that a modern college professor is interested in what goes on in the schools, and, as it happened, when he wrote the early books of the *Institutio* he was giving thought to the education of his own son. What we must expect to find in Quintilian's discussion of education is not, therefore, basic reform or original speculation, it is reasonable judgment, unprejudiced by special pleading, and a coherent overall view of how the separate parts of education can fit together to produce an educated man. What we find also is an unusually sensitive understanding of the child's psychology.

## I  *Primary Education*

Quintilian's first chapter is devoted to the earliest instruction of a child. It is typical of him that he first stresses the naturalness of learning, and that his sympathies are with the child. The child is born to learn as a bird is born for flight, a horse for the race. If a child turns against education, it is the fault of parent or teacher, not of the child. Since this is the case, education should start from the very beginning, but without forcing and in a way as much like play as possible. Furthermore, those who surround a child have influence upon him from the very start, both morally and intellectually.

Among the debated points about primary education were whether the child should begin with Greek or with Latin, and at what age a beginning should be made. Quintilian favors beginning with Greek (I,i,12), but the student should start Latin soon thereafter or he will develop Grecisms in pronunciation and usage. The Stoic writers are correct, he thinks, in saying that study should be started as early as possible (I,i,15–19). There is no need to wait until the traditional age of seven. A child has to do *something;* he might as well start to grow intellectually as well as morally. Any progress that is made will be to the good as long as the child is amused and not embittered. Furthermore, the most important element in early learning is memory, and this is strong in small children. Advantage should be taken of it.

Quintilian's strongest feature here is his psychology, learned possibly from writers on education, more likely from his own sympathy with children. It is this same psychology which makes him object to the custom of teaching children to recite the alphabet without teaching them the shapes of letters (I,i,24). He objects also to indifference to penmanship, apparently on the part of parents rather than teachers (I,i,28). If a child writes poorly, he cannot get his thoughts down efficiently or read them off easily. Good reading habits must be built up from the start, and it is important to avoid haste. Quintilian appreciates what a difficult coordination of skills is involved in reading, for as the eyes move on, the child says one word while looking at the next (I,i,34). Less sound, psychologically, are the recommendations that the child should not practice writing common words, but rare ones, so that he will be improving his vocabulary, and that when he writes whole verses they ought to be morally as well as intellectually improving (I,i,34–35). Greek teachers had used improving maxims from Menander and other writers, and Roman teachers subsequently used the *disticha Catonis* for the same purpose.[4]

Quintilian's discussion of primary education has nothing to say about the primary school, and no word occurs which seems to correspond to the *grammatistes,* the primary teacher in a Greek school, for which *litterator* or *primus magister* or *magister ludi* was sometimes used by Latin writers. Apparently the parents of Quintilian's potential orator prefer to start his education at home. In addition to

his parents, three types of individuals contribute to a child's earliest
education according to Quintilian: nurse, young slaves in the household, and a pedagogue (I,i,11). The nurse is apparently in charge
for roughly the first three years, after which the pedagogue takes
over. Strictly speaking, a pedagogue was a person, often a slave, who
accompanied a child to school, but he was supposed to be a moral
and intellectual force on the child, and from Quintilian's account
(I,i,8; I,ii,10) it seems probable that the pedagogue is in charge of
the child's education from the age of about four until he goes to the
grammarian, which should be as soon as he has facility in reading
and writing. The pedagogue thus becomes an actual teacher for a
few years. Parents are warned that the pedagogue must recognize
his limitations and give up his pupil when the time comes. Presumably the pedagogue then continued as guardian and companion.

## II  *The Grammar School*

This private beginning to studies does not mean that Quintilian
disapproves of schools, though he is aware of dangers of moral corruption at the hands of other boys or masters. Pederasty was common
and acceptable in certain circles, though not to Quintilian, and there
were other dangers. The second chapter of the *Institutio* discusses
the moral and academic arguments against and for schools, as opposed to private study at home. The primary consideration is that
the orator must be a man of action, must be accustomed to people
and to life, and this he will learn best in a school. Quintilian objects
to private education in the same way he later objects to some contemporary declamation, as remote from reality. Furthermore, he sees
an important educational factor in the emulation found in a school,
in hearing others praised or blamed, and in the rivalry of a school,
and he describes with approval the way students were given a
monthly rating in the school which he himself attended (I,ii,23).
It worked especially well on a student with Quintilian's strong sense
of duty. In the following chapter he discusses incentives to learning:
memory and facility at imitation, provided it does not become mimicry, are the best signs of potential ability. Quintilian's ideal pupil
(I,iii,6–7) is one whom praise excites, who delights in success, who
weeps in failure. He feeds on ambition, is stung by reproach, urged
on by honor. In such a one laziness need not be feared. A modern
educator might agree that a boy of this sort would seem easy to
teach, but there is danger that he would regard pleasing the teacher
as his primary goal and thus be led into an attitude of conformity.

The traditional and conservative nature of Roman education did not make conformity seem a danger, and Quintilian's imperial patrons doubtless regarded it as a positive virtue.

Quintilian insists that corporal punishment should not be used (I,iii,13–14). This is one of his most famous educational dicta. He describes beating as servile, insulting, ineffective, and unnecessary. It can do permanent damage to a boy's personality, and it brings out the sadist in the teacher. Beatings were commonplace in ancient primary and grammar schools, but probably not in the rhetorical schools, which of course is where Quintilian himself had taught. Almost the only earlier criticism, and that not so thorough-going, is one remark by Seneca.[5] Quintilian's attitude was doubtless consistent with the humanitarian spirit of the times, and again indicative of his sympathies with children, but had little influence.

The chapters now numbered iv through ix describe the substance of grammar and are chiefly of interest to students of the Latin language. The fact that Quintilian summarizes this material in considerable detail suggests that he had found some students inadequately trained in language. He repeatedly defends the importance, and even pleasure, of studying grammar, but also criticizes the pedantry of some grammarians, and hesitates to make additions to a body of knowledge already overly complex (I,v,17). His good sense and practicality are evident in his treatment of the question of analogy and anomaly which had been debated by grammarians and by amateurs like Julius Caesar for over two centuries (I,vi,4–27). Characteristically, Quintilian will not follow either school as a rigid doctrine in determining the correct grammatical forms to use. Sometimes analogy is helpful in grammar, but some analogies are apparent rather than real, and Latin inflection is not totally systematic. Quintilian thinks the best basis of grammar is usage, not the usage of just anybody, but the consensus of the educated, just as the consensus of the good is a guide to living (I,vi,45).

After describing the science of correct speech, Quintilian turns to the second aspect of grammar, reading. In ancient times literature was usually written to be heard. Thus Quintilian begins with oral reading, but he soon moves on to consider what should be read. He agrees entirely with the custom of reading first Homer in Greek and Virgil in Latin, but other writers may be added, especially comedians like Menander, once the students are grown up enough not to be morally corrupted. Only poets were read in grammar schools. Historically this goes back to the fact that Greek education was older than Greek literary prose, but the custom was perpetuated by the richness of Greek and Latin poetry and its suitability for classroom purposes. Quintilian shows exactly how class discussion is to proceed (I,viii,13–21): a verse is read out, its parts of speech and metrical features identified, each word classified, each trope and figure named, the arrangement of the words noted. In the actual treatment by grammarians the poem tended to be fractured into tiny segments and the thought and overall effect went unappreciated, but Quintilian tries to take a broader view of the whole composition (I,viii, 17). This reading and analysis was called *historike* in Greek, and to a limited extent what we call history entered into it. History was never a discipline in ancient education. Historical allusions in the poets are to be explained fully, but Quintilian warns against wasting time on pedantic digressions on history. What he seems to fear most is the tendency to make exhaustive collections of unreliable alternative accounts of events, a problem which existed also in the treatment of mythology. Indeed, Quintilian draws no line between mythology, as seen for example in the stories of the Trojan War, and history, as seen in the Punic Wars.

Quintilian's grammarian also teaches composition as an introduction to the exercises of the rhetorical schools (I,ix). There are oral exercises, such as retelling of Aesop's fables and paraphrasing of poetry, and short written exercises describing a saying or action with some kind of moral value. Quintilian does not explain the technique very fully, but we know these and other exercises from Greek handbooks of composition called *progymnasmata* such as that published soon after Quintilian's time by Aelius Theon.

The discussion of the grammar school concludes with some remarks on "other arts" which should be taught (I,x). These are part of what the Greeks had called *enkyklios paideia* and became the seven liberal arts of late antiquity and the Middle Ages: grammar, logic, rhetoric, arithmetic, geometry, music, and astronomy. Quintilian does not discuss arithmetic: numbers have been taught by the elementary teachers and the rest of the subject he probably regarded as part of geometry. Logic is regarded as a part of rhetorical argumentation and need not be separately studied. This leaves music, geometry, and astronomy as the arts which Quintilian discusses.

Although the idea of "encyclopedic" study of the liberal arts had been stated in Latin by Varro and Vitruvius, it is not what Quintilian has in mind. He regards grammar and rhetoric as constituting the real substance of education. The other arts cannot make an orator, but since they exist, he cannot, by definition, be perfect without knowledge of them. Quintilian was doubtless influenced by Cicero's claim in *On the Orator* that the orator needed a broad general education, but his description indicates that he regards non-verbal arts as something merely ancillary. He is quite apologetic about requiring them at all and spends most of his time justifying their utility. His arguments sound like commonplaces taken from treatises on music or geometry or astronomy. The general cultural value of these disciplines is acknowledged—geometry for example sharpens the intellect—but Quintilian is concerned to show that all the arts can have a practical utility for the orator. Thus music contributes to the tone or modulation of the voice, geometry to an orator's knowledge of land measurement, astronomy to the need to explain an eclipse. Some of this seems rather farfetched, and its presence indicates that by Roman standards Quintilian was straining to be broad in his view of the curriculum. The unusual scope of the *Institutio* has made it possible for him to view education as a whole, which the grammarian did not do, and thus led him to acknowledge the value of some topics which were not well integrated into the ordinary course of studies.

Although grammar and music had once been united and taught by the same teacher, this was no longer done (I,X,17). Apparently a student is to be sent to special masters for each art (I,xii,6 and 13), though of course the grammarian may himself need a knowledge of these subjects in elucidating particular passages in the poets. The student should also have instruction in delivery from an actor (I,xi, 1–14) and a moderate amount of physical training in the palaestra will do him no harm (I,xi,15–19).

The last chapter of Book I again shows that Quintilian's picture of education at this level seemed to him rather daring, for he reassures his readers that there is time for all these studies, that the young mind really can absorb them. One subject refreshes after another, and the student is ready to learn. Further, one who is determined to be a great orator must put aside the temptations of leisure, shows, games, sleep, and banquets and keep before him eloquence, the queen of all things. The passage has been criticized on the ground that Quintilian seems to blame the laziness of pupils when the fault is that they are not afforded the right instruction by teachers or parents.[6] His intention, however, is not to blame the young but to exhort the adult world.

It seems likely, then, that Quintilian's enlargement of the scope of the *Institutio* led him to some remarks on education which, though hardly very original, since they were modeled on suggestions in Cicero and other writers, yet departed somewhat from ordinary Roman practice. We have no evidence what disciplines other than rhetoric the elder Pliny included in his work, *The Student*, though his own studies were of course very wide. The writings of Roman grammarians never say anything about subjects other than grammar, and none of the grammarians discussed by Suetonius in his history of the subject seems to have concerned himself with anything but grammar in the narrow sense.[7]

### III   *The Rhetorical School*

A second result of the scope of the *Institutio* is that it leads Quintilian to consider the transition from the grammatical to the rhetorical school, a subject on which he seems to have had strong personal feelings. In discussing composition in the grammar school, he says (I,ix,6) that Latin rhetoricians have neglected to teach some of the intermediate exercises in composition and that grammarians have necessarily taken them over, something which has not happened in the Greek schools. The subject is discussed again more extensively in the first chapter of the second book, where it appears that both groups have been at fault: the rhetoricians think that exercises other than deliberative and judicial declamation, *suasoriae* and *controversiae*, are beneath them; the grammarians have not only rightly taken over neglected intermediate exercises, like those described in the fourth chapter of the book, but have even tried to take over the teaching of *suasoriae*. Quintilian's objection is based on his concept of grammar and rhetoric. Each has its own function and ought not to do the work of the other. Rhetoricians should teach those exercises like narrations or laudations or commonplaces which can be a part of an actual deliberative or judicial speech. There is no reason why a student's work with grammarians and rhetoricians cannot overlap (II,i,12–13). We know that grammar and rhetoric, in earlier times, were taught successfully by the same person. Quintilian admits that some grammarians may be able to go beyond their subject, but they should realize that they are teaching rhetoric when they do so (II, i,6). Rhetoric is a great subject to Quintilian and must not be loosely treated. One of the objectives of the *Institutio* is to show that greatness.

Quintilian's remark that because of the realignment of grammar and rhetoric, students were going to the rhetorician at a more advanced age than reason demanded is something which we might not have guessed. Romans sometimes give the impression of having started rhetoric in the cradle. There was apparently no set age to begin. Cicero was studying rhetoric in 92 B.C. when he was fourteen, and possibly he had begun earlier than that. His nephew Quintus was very enthusiastic about rhetoric at thirteen or fourteen.[8] Augustus delivered a funeral oration for his aunt when eleven and Tiberius one for his father when nine;[9] although they probably did not write them themselves, they must have been given training in memory and delivery. Nero was about thirteen when he became Seneca's pupil, and rhetoric was perhaps part of his studies at the time. Really we have little evidence, but if Quintilian is correct that boys were going to the rhetorician at a later age, we may guess that this meant about fifteen rather than thirteen or fourteen. Pliny the Younger first spoke in the law courts at eighteen and need not have begun rhetoric until he was fifteen.[10]

Quintilian has not only a high regard for rhetoric, he has a high standard for teachers of rhetoric. People are wrong if they think a teacher of inferior ability is suitable for giving the first instruction in rhetoric on the ground that an expert will not trouble himself with elementary points. A student should go to the best teacher from the very beginning (II,iii). Quintilian's best teacher is best in his knowledge and practice of rhetoric, best in a moral sense, but also best in his knowledge of boys and understanding of the educational process. There is a mutual responsibility of the teacher to play a role like that of a parent and of a student to regard a teacher as a father, not of his body, but of his mind (II,ix,1). It is in discussion of such subjects as this that Quintilian shows the sensitive gentleness which has been often admired in him. What he says seems common sense, commonly ignored. For example, consider this passage on the duty of teachers:

Above all, the teacher should assume toward his students the attitude of a parent and he should regard himself as having stepped into the place of those from whom the children came to him. He should have no vices himself nor tolerate them in others. His strictness ought not to be grim, nor his fellowship unrestrained: the former produces dislike, the latter contempt. He should have much to say about what is honorable and good, for the more often he admonishes, the rarer will he censure. He should not be easily provoked, but neither should he wear a fair face toward what ought to be corrected. He should be straightforward in teaching, hardworking, persistent rather than excessive. He should willingly answer those who question him and himself question those who do not. In praising the work of his pupils he ought to be neither stingy nor effusive, because the one begets discouragement and the other overconfidence. In criticizing what needs correction, he should not be sarcastic nor at all abusive, for many are frightened off from their course of study by the fact that some-one finds fault with them as though he hates them. The teacher himself should have something to say, should even have much to say, which his hearers will remember. Although there are enough examples for imitation to be found in reading, still, the living voice, as it is called, gives fuller nourishment and especially the voice of a teacher whom pupils both love and respect if they have been rightly educated. One can hardly exaggerate how enthusiastically we imitate those whom we favor. (II,ii,4–8)

From Quintilian's approach to education, we would expect his discussion of the rhetorical school to be more personal perhaps than his account of the grammar school, but not aimed at making funda-mental changes in Roman practice, and this is true. Among the points he makes strongly enough to suggest that they involve some de-parture from ordinary custom are these: boys should be sent to the rhetorician at an earlier age (II,i); boys should not applaud each other's declamations in class, for it is the judgment of the teacher that matters (II,ii,9–12); in the classroom younger and older boys should not sit mixed in together, since it makes discipline difficult (II,ii,14); boys should be sent to the best possible teachers (II,iii,1); students should ordinarily memorize select passages from great authors rather than their own compositions (II,vii). More funda-mental are Quintilian's suggestions about reading and about decla-mation.

Reading in the rhetorical schools is the subject of what is now the fifth chapter of Book II. First of all, since he has already said that students should go to the rhetorician at an early age, Quintilian thinks it would be a good idea if they could continue analytical reading not entirely unlike what they had been doing with the gram-marian, but now concentrating on historians, especially Livy, and orators, especially Cicero. He says he had tried this in his own school, but had to give it up. Custom was against the whole thing, and most of his students were older and had no need of such instruction: they had come to him to study declamation.

It was thus not so much the reading classes which failed as Quin-tilian's attempt to get younger boys to begin rhetoric. Modern parents are attracted by college programs of early admission. Ancient parents were not, and not even the most distinguished educator of the day, with the stamp of approval of the emperor himself, could effect much change in Roman practice. Quintilian goes on to say that Greek rhetorical schools, which he had earlier said took younger pupils, did have reading classes, usually conducted by assistant masters, but the work in these classes was too elementary. He then describes (II, v,6–9) the kind of rhetorical, as opposed to grammatical, analysis which he thinks appropriate to accompany reading in elementary stages of the rhetorical schools. Both flaws and virtues are to be pointed out; questions must be asked and the student's judgment developed, "for what is our object in teaching them except that they may not always have to be taught?" (II,v,13).

In chapters vi through ix of Book II, Quintilian is still discussing instruction of the novice in rhetoric. From a passage later in the work (VIII,pr.,1–5) we learn that a special brief course of lectures in rhetorical theory was given to beginning students of rhetoric; subsequently the same ground was covered again in greater detail. The novice needs special assistance in composition (II,vi,5); he should memorize passages from great speeches or histories and only rarely his own compositions (II,vii); the teacher must carefully study his abilities to see what kind of treatment he needs (II,viii). But finally the time comes when the pupil is ready for declamation of deliberative and judicial themes (II,x,1). From here on the curriculum will consist of two things, systematic lectures on rhetorical theory and the composition and delivery of declamations. Perhaps Quintilian wants the student in his school to read continually on his own, but he doesn't say so. When he again gets around to the subject of reading, it is a program designed for the student who has learned enough theory and practice to prepare him to make the step to real lawsuits (X,i,4). Most rhetoricians probably thought that rhetorical theory and declamation were more than enough to keep a student busy.

## IV  Declamation

The real emphasis of contemporary rhetorical education was on declamation, and more on *controversiae*, or judicial declamation, than on *suasoriae*, deliberative exercises, which were regarded as easier. Declamation was occasionally criticized as artificial and impractical, but with little effect.[11] To Quintilian there is no question of its importance and utility: it includes all the material of all other exercises and it comes close to actual oratory (II,x,2). Or it ought to. But students have been allowed to declaim on bizarre subjects, including declamations involving magicians, plagues, oracles, cruel stepmothers, and the like, and they have been allowed to handle the subjects in a swollen and artificial style. Later in the work, he points out a number of ways in which conventions of the schools have bad effects on oratory in the courts, as when the judge is assumed to be familiar with the case in the same way that an audience knows the theme of declamation (IV,i,3), or in the insertion of an inappropriate digression for display (IV,iii,2–3), or in the ignoring of objections, or the making of unwarranted assumptions.[12] In an elaborate passage in Book V, he develops a comparison between declamation oriented toward display and lacking the strength of argument and proof and the soft, enervated, specious prettiness of eunuchs.[13] Some specific suggestions are made to try to bring declamation back into line as a training for the courts (II,x,9). Quintilian thinks that proper names should be used, presumably instead of types like the soldier, the father, the maiden. Types had apparently been introduced in the early first century B.C. as a way to universalize examples.[14] Second, the cases should be more complicated and require more extensive speeches.[15] More normal diction should also be used and so should humor.

As regards the themes, Quintilian's suggestion must not be exaggerated. He wants to get rid of some of the fantastic characters, but he does not mean to limit the subjects to such humdrum cases as actually made up most legal dockets. The cases had to awaken the boys' interests. Some instances of themes which Quintilian seems to approve appear in the course of the work, for example:

Some young men who were accustomed to enjoy each other's company decided to have a picnic on the seashore. Since one could not come, they raised a mound and inscribed his name on it. [Later] his father landed on that very shore from a voyage abroad, read the name, and hanged himself. The young men are alleged to be the cause of his death.

This much is the theme of the declamation; Quintilian continues with a discussion of treatment:

It is the definition of the prosecution that a person through whom it has been brought about that someone dies is the cause of his death. The defense replies that it is someone who knowingly does something through which it necessarily results that a man dies. Apart from the definition, it is enough for the prosecutor to say "you were the cause of death. Through you it resulted that a man died, because unless you had done what you did he would be alive." In reply it may be said that a person through whom it resulted that someone died ought not to be convicted out of hand.

This would apply to a prosecutor, a witness, and a judge in a capital case. Blame does not always inhere in the cause of a course of actions, for example if someone urged a trip or summoned a friend from across the sea and he died in shipwreck, or invited someone to dinner who then died of overeating. The action of the young men was not the sole cause of death; the credulity of the old man and his weakness in bearing grief were also involved. In short, if he had been stronger or wiser, he would be alive. They did not act with evil intent, and the father could have guessed from the position of the mound or the hasty way it was built that it was not a tomb. . . . (VII,iii,30–34)

This is much like themes for declamation in the writings of Seneca the Elder, and it is perhaps typical of what Quintilian used in his school. When a rhetorician proposed a theme, he sometimes made comments on its treatment, and Quintilian's remarks here are of that sort. The students were usually allowed to choose which side to support and whether to speak as an advocate or a principal. They ordinarily wrote their speeches out, then delivered them from memory.

The situation in this particular theme is an improbable one, but the characters involved do not give much occasion for exotic treatment. At most, a declaimer for the prosecution could develop the grief of the father, or a speaker for the defense his senility. Quintilian here has not followed his own advice that characters should have names or that cases should be made complicated, but in Book III,vi,96–97, he cites a complicated theme in an inheritance case involving six different laws, and in Book V he gives a theme which does have specific names:

When Alexander sacked Thebes, he found some records which stated that the Thebans had loaned a hundred talents to the Thessalians. Since the Thessalians had been his allies, he gave them the tablets as a gift. Later, after the Thebans had been restored by Cassander, they demanded the money back from the Thessalians. The case is tried before the Amphictyonic Council. It is agreed that the Thebans had loaned a hundred talents and not been repaid. The whole controversy revolves around the point that Alexander is said to have made a gift of the talents to the Thessalians. It is further agreed that no money was given them by Alexander; the question is therefore whether the gift he made is substantially the same as if he had given money. (V,x,111–112)

Two collections of declamations attributed to Quintilian have been preserved in manuscripts.[16] One, known as the *Declamationes*

*Maiores,* consists of nineteen full-scale declamations. The themes involve stepmothers, soothsayers, pirates, pestilences, potions, and the like, and the style is not that of Quintilian. It seems unlikely that he had anything to do with them. The other collection, *Declamationes Minores,* now consists of one hundred and forty-five of what were originally three hundred and eighty-eight brief declamations or selections from declamations. A considerable number of them are accompanied by brief advice on the rhetorical treatment to be used. Four of these declamations involve pestilences and oracles, and there are a few cruel stepmothers, but there are no magicians at all. Most of the themes are rather practical, and the style is not unlike Quintilian's. It is possible that this collection derives, at least in part, from Quintilian or his school. If so, both the examples of declamation in the *Institutio* and the *Declamationes Minores* may be taken to suggest that exercises assigned by Quintilian were intended to be practical and rather restrained, but were not fundamentally different from those of other rhetoricians.

Early in the chapter we said that Quintilian's influence in education was on the side of making it more humane, more moral, more practical, somewhat more profound, slightly broader. Examples of all these qualities have been given. There was nothing radical about his educational theory, and some of the improvements which he recommended he could not put into practice. This is not an indictment of him so much as a reflection of the adherence to the status quo in Roman society. Extensive revision in the curriculum, which may seem desirable to us, was unthinkable. The worst that can be said about Roman education is that it did service to an outworn ideal and ignored not only the scientist and the technician as it always had, but also many of the special needs of future public administrators and bureaucrats who in practice replaced the orator at the heart of public life and whose training throughout the empire came largely from rhetoricians. From the vantage point of modern education it would seem that they needed training in economics and sociology, in regional studies, including history and religion, in accounting and business methods, and in many other subjects which did not exist. Yet somehow they managed. The best that can be said about Roman education is that it emphasized ingenuity, an imaginative response to a verbal problem, and a kind of colorful, if often superficial, originality. Though it began with rote memorization, it ended by trying to create literature. For all the rhetoricians' rules and lists, there does not seem to have been a right or wrong treatment of a declamation. They taught neither facts nor discipline so much as art.

As a state official Quintilian may have exercised some influence on other rhetorical schools, but there is no sign of this, or of direct educational influence in the centuries immediately following his death. In the Renaissance, however, he was discovered, and many a subsequent educator has found with satisfaction some cherished theory of his own anticipated in the *Institutio*. This continues to be the case in the twentieth century, where Quintilian enjoys a secure place in the study of the history of education, chiefly because of his discussion of elementary education.

# CHAPTER 4

## *Quintilian on Rhetoric*

QUINTILIAN'S account of rhetorical theory extends from the eleventh chapter of Book II through the end of Book XI, dealing first with general questions, then with the separate parts of rhetoric: invention, arrangement, style, memory, and delivery. Although no surviving earlier work follows exactly this system, we know that it was a standard approach.[1] Throughout the discussion Quintilian's account has certain persistent features: his moral outlook is intensive and only in a few passages is there any compromise with expediency; he pursues a natural order and often concerns himself with the relation between nature and art; he frequently takes a historical view and presents a variety of opinions, criticizes them, and chooses among them; he follows no single rhetorical school or sect, and implies that he has read widely in writers on rhetoric, but the influence of Cicero is very strong. There are many references to the rhetorical theory of *On the Orator* and *The Orator* and to other works of Cicero and there are more illustrations of technique taken from Cicero's speeches than from any other source. Yet Quintilian does not hesitate to disagree with Cicero on theoretical points, and his rhetoric cannot be regarded as a Ciceronian revival pure and simple.[2] Although there are often signs of the influence of rhetorical writers subsequent to Cicero, the only ones frequently named are Apollodorus and Theodorus, whose trivialities Quintilian dislikes, Cornelius Celsus,[3] with whom he usually disagrees, and his old teacher, Domitius Afer, whom he praises. Since it is against his custom to refer by name to living writers, he may be following or rejecting contemporary rhetoricians unknown to us as he chooses between various rhetorical doctrines (III,i,21). Occasionally he points out his own originality on some matter, thus tempting us to believe that he otherwise is following some authority, even if unspecified, but in the case of topics like comparison he may have taken a final logical step toward a conclusion without entirely realizing his own contribution. His good sense is repeatedly evident in his refusal to be dogmatic on debated issues: rules are useful, but we must follow what is becoming and what is expedient in adapting ourselves to the case and occasion and we must not go to extremes. The need for judgment, he felt, was one of the reasons why rhetoric was a great and difficult art. Particularly in matters of style does he stress the need to avoid fads.

Again, it is typical of Quintilian that the theories he advances are meant to be practical. Though he often mentions declamation or uses themes from declamation as illustrations, he points out that some conventions of the schoolroom do not work well in actual courts of law, where the speaker must influence a real judge or jury and cannot indulge artistic whims. He wants a student to learn how to argue and persuade, not only how to adorn and entertain, and when he discusses such things as humor or the devices of style, he never fails to consider them from a practical viewpoint as techniques of persuasion. Similarly, he never forgets that he is a teacher, and we shall see him tailor theory to students' needs, as in his discussion of memory, or suggest an alternative approach of educational value, as in the case of stasis theory. In comparison with many rhetoricians he is restrained in the classification and subdivision of topics, something which had gained ground steadily since the beginnings of rhetoric in the fifth century B.C. and threatened to crush the whole study under technical terms. Indeed, technical terms seem to be uncongenial to him, a factor which occasionally detracts from his clarity. All of these qualities will emerge if we analyze Quintilian's discussion of rhetoric part by part.

## I  The Nature of Rhetoric

In the initial discussion of rhetoric which takes up the second half of Book II, Quintilian is concerned with certain general matters relating to almost everything he will subsequently say. Many of them had been repeatedly discussed since the beginning of the rhetorical consciousness in fifth century Greece. The topic with which Quintilian begins is a fundamental one, the question of whether rules are necessary at all, whether a man cannot speak without them. Though the problem was a traditional one, Quintilian is clearly combating some contemporaries; first (II,xi), teachers of rhetoric who neglect theory and are only interested in declamation, and particularly in showy display. The picture of declaimers in Seneca, Petronius, and other writers is consistent enough to confirm the reality of such a viewpoint; Quintilian does not so much refute it as reject it out of hand, since it produces speeches which are incoherent in an over-all sense and inartistic. A second group (II,xii) he opposes are largely not teachers, but practicing orators who scorn theory and yet are continually praised for their vigor. To Quintilian, what they display is not vigor, but uncontrolled violence. From the account of imperial oratory in Tacitus' *Dialogue* it seems clear that a considerable number of the most famous orators from the time of Cassius Severus to that of Tacitus and Quintilian belonged to this group, and both from what Tacitus says and what Quintilian himself says subsequently (II,xx,2), they are particularly to be associated with opportunistic, unscrupulous, rhetorically untrained, informers.[4] Quintilian opposes their moral ambivalence as well as their lack of theory, but he does so cautiously, without directly labeling anyone an informer. Domitian could be expected to be sensitive on this subject.

After having disposed of both of these groups, Quintilian can give his own view of rhetorical rules (II,xiii): they are not absolutes, but guidelines to be adapted by the skilled speaker to individual time and place. As reasonable as this seems, it was necessary to say, since some rhetorical schools dogmatically insisted upon the absolute applicability of certain requirements, the Apollodoreans for example upon the formal parts of a speech in canonical order in every oration. To Quintilian, rules can never suffice totally to deal with the greatness of the art:

The orator's task is extensive and diverse and almost constantly novel and one about which everything will never be said. Yet I shall try to recount what has been handed down and what of this seems best and anything that will be better changed, added, or subtracted. (II,xiii,17)

Quintilian is now ready to turn to the term "rhetoric" and its definition. After explaining the problems involved in adapting the Greek term "rhetoric" into Latin, he inserts that division of his subject into art, artificer, and work which we have already mentioned (II,xiv,5). That it was not a fundamental part of his thinking might be concluded from his failure to state it in the preface to Book I where he blocked out the plan of his work. It seems to have been suggested here by the fact that terms like "rhetoric," "eloquence," and "oratorical" refer variously to the theory of speech or to its manifestation in speech or to a speaker himself.

The chapter on the definition of rhetoric follows Quintilian's basic method of reviewing and choosing or adapting what seems to him the best. Greek definitions of rhetoric as the artificer of persuasion are rejected since other things than rhetoric can persuade, money for example, and if the words "by speaking" are added they restrict rhetoric too narrowly to successful persuasion. Nor is Aristotle's celebrated definition satisfactory, which Quintilian quotes rather freely as "the power of discovering everything persuasive in a speech" (II, xv,13), for this might be taken to include the appeals of prostitutes, flatterers, and corrupters, and it limits rhetoric to invention. To Quintilian, it is axiomatic that an orator must be a good man, a point which he had made in the first book, which he refers to here and in the following chapters, and which he further develops in Book XII. The point doubtless seemed an especially significant one in an age in which the most powerful orators were often the vicious informers. Quintilian's final definition, "the science of speaking well" (II,xv,34), as he says, is substantially the definition of the Stoic philosophers Cleanthes and Chrysippus, "the science of speaking rightly." "Well" thus means morally right. In the course of Quintilian's treatment, it is also taken to mean artistically right, but it does not necessarily mean successfully, and the name of orator cannot be denied to a man just because he loses his case. The word "science" is used rather generally to mean a body of knowledge; Quintilian certainly does not mean that rhetoric deals with certainties, for he seems to think of "science" and "virtue," that is, a good quality in a man, as much the same thing (II,xv,36), and in succeeding chapters he equates rhetoric with an art and again with virtue. The many arguments for and against the artistic nature of rhetoric which had accumulated over the centuries are recapitulated (II, xvii). As an art, it is useful and good (II,xvi) and also an active or practical thing, a method, though it has some of the contemplative and some of the productive about it (II,xviii). Its material exists in nature, but can only be made perfect by art (II,xix). To show that it is a virtue, basically a Stoic position, Quintilian claims an original proof (II,xx,5–8): an orator cannot praise unless he knows what is honorable, he cannot persuade unless he knows what is advantageous, he cannot speak in court unless he knows what is just. He often needs courage to speak at all. Thus the virtues of justice, prudence, and fortitude are needed by the orator and his art itself becomes a virtue. Finally (II,xxi), rhetoric deals with whatever material is brought under its notice for discussion, not solely with politics or legal matters. In the resolution of this old dispute, one can see the influences with had carried rhetoric from a rather nar-rowly defined technique, successful in the Greek law courts, to an alternative to philosophy, embracing all of literature and most of life, independent of practical success, expressive of the nature of man. Quintilian's definition adequately describes rhetoric as he under-stood it.

## II  *Invention*

Book III, like the last part of Book II, deals with somewhat general matters: the history and parts of rhetoric, but in discussing them Quintilian has already entered into the traditional topic of invention. He claims that he will be fuller on all these subjects than many have been, and that it is here that his friends are especially anxious for his opinion, since those who have discussed these subjects are in disagreement (III,i,1–2). Rhetoricians apparently felt very strongly about the number and names of the parts of rhetoric, the duties of the orator, the kinds of speeches, the classification of questions (III, i,5–6). Quintilian's views on these topics are sensible, but he keeps to the traditional lines. To a modern reader the most significant problem is probably that involving the kinds of speeches. Quintilian says (III,iv,12) that it is "safest and most reasonable" to follow the majority of authors and to distinguish three kinds, though he notes that the most famous expert of his time had followed the suggestion of Cicero that there were innumerable different kinds (III,iv,2). Who this is we do not know. Quintilian's three kinds are those of Aristotle: laudative, deliberative, and judicial. Declamation is provided for, since any of the three may be used for serious business or for show (III,iv,14).

Those who attacked this threefold classification alleged that it had described the chief kinds of speeches of classical Greece, but no longer suited (III,iv,4). In fact, the nature of oratory had changed somewhat, and opportunities for traditional deliberative oratory especially had declined because of changes in the constitution and probably because of some loss of freedom of speech. Quintilian does not directly comment on any aspect of this problem, least of all the last. He believed that the three categories of oratory were sound because every speech was judicial or not, and if not judicial involved either praising or blaming the past or deliberating about the future, a view which is not quite the same as that of Aristotle.[5]

At the same time he shows some tendency in other parts of his work to redefine deliberative oratory to include more than speeches in the senate and assemblies. "There seems to me," he says "a greater variety in this field than has been recognized, for there are many kinds of advisers and advice" (III,viii,15). Back in Book II (xvi,19) he had described the function of an orator as the defense of his friends, the advising of the senate and people, or the encouragement of an army. The latter may be classified as deliberative by Quintilian's definition, for it is non-judicial and deals with future action. It was certainly a field of oratory which offered some opportunities, but which had not been discussed by rhetoricians and is known mostly from the speeches in historians. It reappears in the description of the perfect orator in Book XII (i,28), and the military orator thus seems a definite part of Quintilian's view of rhetoric. Possibly the events of A.D. 69 had brought the matter forcibly to his attention. Poetry and history are of course good sources of oratorical examples, and Quintilian recognizes that rhetoric is a preparation for the writing of deliberative speeches in poems and histories (III,viii,49).

Another extension of the field of deliberative oratory is to speeches of advice to friends and to the emperor (III,viii,70). The latter was occasionally a possibility, to judge again from examples in histories[6] or from the works of Greek sophists like Dio Chrysostom and Aristeides. Quintilian touches on some aspects of the subject again in Book XII; here these various extensions of the field seem rather incidental, and when deliberative oratory is discussed in detail it is identified primarily not with practical speeches, but with the *suasoriae* common in the schools of declamation where the young of Rome vied with each other to advise Alexander the Great or Hannibal or Cicero about what they ought to do.

The categories which are given most extensive discussion by Quintilian in Book III, and those which probably most interested his friends, relate to questions and stasis, and it is to these that he turns before taking up the separate kinds of oratory in greater detail. *Quaestio*, or question, the subject of chapter v, meant any topic on which two or more opinions could be advanced. It might be of a general sort, such as a philosophical question, or it might be particular, involving specific persons, places, and times, as did questions in courts of law or in political debates. Rhetoricians were chiefly concerned with particular questions, usually called "causes," but Quintilian insists that a particular question logically involves a general question (III,v,9): to decide whether Cato should marry, we have to have decided whether any man should marry.

Stasis was a system of dealing with the problem presented by a question. It had been developed chiefly by the Hellenistic Greek rhetorician Hermagoras and subsequently became very popular among teachers of rhetoric.[7] The system was intended to be an educational technique, a formula to teach a student how to find his strongest point either in attack or defense and how to insure a systematic presentation of his material. Though Hermagoras' general approach prevailed, there were apparently nearly as many variants as there were rhetoricians, for teachers differed acrimoniously about the number and arrangement of the parts of the system and the technical terms to be used. The idea was that a student must first discover the basic issue in a case, which was called in Greek *stasis*, in Latin *constitutio* by earlier writers, *status* in Quintilian's time. According to Quintilian (III,vi,5), the stasis is not the first conflict of opinion, as had sometimes been said, but the issue which arises from the first conflict: "you did it"; "I didn't"; the issue in fact, "did he do it?" In practice an individual speech may contain more than one issue: "it was just to do it, but in fact I didn't."

Quintilian describes systems which distinguish *staseis* varying in number from one to eight. His own system is in the mainstream of rhetorical teaching as seen in Hermagoras and Cicero, and what is unique about it comes from his desire for logical consistency and pedagogical effectiveness. While teaching in his school, he had expounded a view of the subject which he has subsequently come to believe is not entirely accurate, and thus he is at pains to explain that his account in the *Institutio* differs from what his former pupils had heard him say (III,vi,63–65). Like Hippocrates, the teacher of medicine, he is not ashamed to admit that he has been wrong.

The system which Quintilian now accepts, though not described with perfect lucidity, appears to be as follows: the question at issue in a speech may be classified not only as definite or indefinite, but as involving provisions of law or not involving the law. The latter kind of question is "rational," or characterized by reasoning. A question involving reasoning has one of three kinds of stasis: one is dependent on fact, one on definition, and one on quality. These may be seen in the defenses: "I did not do it"; "what I did is not what is charged"; "I was right to do it." A legal question falls under four species: a question of word and intent, a question of contradictory law, a question of syllogism, which means reasoning extending a law to a situation specifically unprovided for, and a question of ambiguous law. But a feature, and apparently a unique feature, of Quintilian's system is that these legal questions are also regarded as reducible to the same three *staseis* as are questions of reasoning.[8] Thus, if the speaker insists on *what* the law literally says, he is using stasis of fact; if he insists on its *spirit,* he is using quality, and either of these in a particular case might involve stasis of definition.

An additional feature of Quintilian's account is that after describing his system of stasis he restates it in a way he hopes will be more useful to a student, though slightly less logically rigorous, "an easier and more open road" (III,vi,83). He begins this version by saying that the strongest answer to a charge is to deny it completely: "I did not do it." The student should take this line if he possibly can. If he cannot answer in this way, the student must deny that the particular charge is applicable: "I did not steal, but took my own property." If this cannot be done, the student will say, "I did it justly." If none of these can be substantiated, the student must try to help his client by finding some flaw in the legal procedure, for example by saying that the case is brought before the wrong court. Many rhetoricians called this technique stasis of exception, and Quintilian himself had once done so, but had come to the conclusion that exception was not a kind of stasis, and might itself contain both rational and legal questions and status of fact, definition, or quality (III,vi,68–77). Logically then it is a different sort of thing, but pedagogically it is convenient to bring it in here.

These four defenses Quintilian here labels "forms of action," but he says that in his early erroneous system he used to call them general bases or *staseis.* They are each divisible into rational or legal questions *(causae).* Legal questions are of various species, such as intent vs. letter, and rational questions too can apparently be classified, for example into questions of quantity, number, relation, or comparison, but this idea is not clearly developed (III,vi,90 and 75). All causes are finally classifiable into three kinds of stasis: conjecture, definition, and quality, as before, but this time Quintilian thinks it is helpful for students to keep stasis derived from legal questions distinct from that in rational questions, and instead of insisting on the logical necessity of three and only three kinds of stasis, he creates three *simulacra,* or counterparts (III,vi,88), of legal stasis exactly parallel to the three rational *staseis.* The system is really a reasonably clear one, though no modern critic seems to have understood it. One reason is that the terminology of forms of action, species of question, and stasis is not too well defined.

An important problem involving stasis was whether or not the system could be applied to all three kinds of oratory. Quintilian believed it could, and this is why he has placed the discussion here before examining the separate kinds. Now he is ready to devote a chapter to each. Laudatory oratory is first examined. Greek theories had been given relatively little adaptation to Roman conditions, for there was little true epideictic at Rome. Often praise or blame became a part of a deliberative or judicial speech. The most characteristic Roman form, funeral oratory, was so traditional and non-literary that the rhetoricians only mention its existence and pass on. In the empire, however, occasions for praising an emperor, alive or dead, regularly arose. A speech of thanks, for example, was given for each pair of consuls, and there were often six pairs a year. A much elaborated example is the panegyric of Trajan which Quintilian's pupil, the younger Pliny, was destined to deliver. There was also the praise of Jupiter which Domitian had made a part of his Capitoline games.[9] As we will see in the final chapter, Greek epideictic entered a new flourishing period about this time and had some influence on Quintilian and other Romans. In Quintilian's view, the arrangement of laudatory speeches can be either chronological or topical (III,vii,15). He rejects the teaching of Celsus that faults can be expressed as virtues, rashness for example as bravery, for this would not befit the good orator (III,vii,25). All three kinds of stasis may occur, but quality will be the commonest.

An ethical problem also arose in connexion with deliberative oratory. Quintilian is very hesitant to accept expediency as the principal basis of argument in deliberation, as Aristotle had claimed. Like Cicero, he fears the separation of the honorable and the expedient.[10] Ethical considerations always figured prominently in Roman oratory, and action purely on a rational basis was not publicly acceptable, as it had once been in Greece. He also objects to necessity as a deliverative topic, though possibility is acceptable (III,viii,22 and 25). The form of a deliberative speech is rather variable, since neither an exordium nor a narration is always necessary (III,viii,6 and 10). The emotional and ethical elements are strong. All kinds of stasis occur, for sometimes the deliberation is about a fact, for example, whether the Pomptine marshes can be drained, often about a quality, as whether or not something is advantageous, occasionally about definition, as in a famous speech by Demosthenes on whether

Philip should "give" or "give back" Halonnesus to Athens (III,viii,5). As we have already said, throughout this chapter Quintilian has declamation chiefly in mind, though nominally as a preparation for giving advice to friends, senate, or emperor.

In discussing judicial oratory Quintilian says that most rhetoricians have thought that a speech has five divisions: exordium, narration, proof, refutation, and peroration (III,ix,1). From the list of parts he rejects partition and proposition, which some added, on the ground that though they occur, they are subdivisions of proof, and he will not accept digression, common as it is, for it is either irrelevant or an ornament to one of the other parts. On the other hand, he does insist that proof and refutation are two essentially different things. Books IV, V, and VI contain Quintilian's ample discussion of the five parts. The end result is to make the *Institutio*, like other ancient rhetorical treatises, a work concerned more than anything else with judicial oratory, among which we must include *controversiae*.

One of the acrimonious differences between the school of the Apollodoreans and that of the Theodoreans involved the question of whether all the major parts must always occur in a speech, and if so whether in the same order.[11] Quintilian's position here is characteristic of him: he does not lightly throw aside the basic parts. Most judicial speeches will contain them and only occasionally can they be omitted. For example, occasionally the judge will need no preparation or time will be lacking for an exordium (IV,i,72–75); the narration can often be brief and sometimes omitted if the facts are known (IV,ii,4–8); the only part that is certainly always needed is the proof (V,*pr.*,5). On the other hand, he is not at all insistent on the traditional order of the parts or the subdivision of them. Nature will show us what to say first, what next (IV,i,52), and nature may dictate an unusual order of the major parts, as in Cicero's greatly admired speech for Milo (IV,ii,24–25). In planning his speech, an orator will usually be well advised to start with the proof, but when he sets out to write a draft he should start with the exordium and work his way through the whole speech in the order in which it is to be delivered (III,ix,8–9).

This is what Quintilian then proceeds to do. He devotes what are now the last two chapters of Book III to the preliminary categorizations which the orator should make in his mind; he is then ready to begin discussion of the exordium at the beginning of Book IV. For the sake of completeness, the categorizations are presented in the full technical manner of Hermagoras, but Quintilian makes it clear that in practice he regards such concern with terminological minutiae as pedantic and unnecessary.

Although much of the material in Quintilian's discussion of the parts of a judicial oration is highly traditional and can be found in the *Rhetoric to Herennius* or in Cicero and probably was also set forth by Celsus and other writers, there are a number of passages which are unique or of some special interest. For example, Quintilian's basic concept of the exordium as directed toward making the audience well disposed, attentive, and teachable is quite standard, though he perhaps plays down slightly the theory of the *insinuatio*, or subtle approach, needed when the orator faces special prejudice or difficulty (IV,i,42–50). On the other hand, he recognizes one point which had been ignored by many rhetoricians: the possibility of making effective use of the character of the patron or pleader separately from the character of the client.[12] This had ordinarily been impossible in Greek oratory where a litigant pleaded his own case even though he employed the help of a professional speech writer. Cicero on the other hand capitalized on the separation of pleader and litigant even to the point of contrasting what his client wanted him to say.[13] Quintilian also recognizes how much easier it is for a patron to praise his client than for a litigant to praise himself (IV, i,45–46).

Another feature of the chapter, very characteristic of Quintilian, is that the discussion of the theory of the exordium is followed by a brief attempt to show a student how he should set to work to compose an exordium (IV,i,52–79), just as the theory of stasis was followed by an illustration of how to apply it.

The next chapter is a long, but well-written discussion of the narration, much of it concerned with the traditional requirements that it be clear, brief, and credible. Quintilian is at pains to show that the Theodorean school is wrong in thinking clarity and brevity sometimes unnecessary (IV,ii,32). He also introduces a discussion of "colors," the explanations adopted by orators to justify or explain something, often involving a certain amount of clever fiction and chiefly to be found in the rhetorical schools (IV,ii,88–100). The last three chapters of Book IV glance at the three oratorical features which some rhetoricians had labeled parts, but which Quintilian prefers to think of in connection with other parts: digression, proposition, and partition. Digression, he says (IV,iii,2), is only too often an unsuitable carry-over into the law courts from the displays of the schools of declamation.

In Book V comes the discussion of the real heart of a speech, the proof. Quintilian claims to follow Aristotle in making a fundamental division of proof into inartificial and artificial, or direct evidence and argument (V,i,1). The former consists of previous court judgments about aspects of the particular case, public opinion about the case, the evidence of slaves given under torture, documents, oaths, and witnesses. In most cases these are not adequate in themselves, but become the basis of arguments. Although each is discussed, Quintilian points out (V,i,3) that he is deliberately brief and has avoided listing the various commonplaces which can be used. Since direct evidence played almost no part in declamation, the subject had not been much studied by rhetoricians.

By far the most interesting section of Quintilian's discussion of direct evidence is the chapter on the examination of witnesses, for it is the only surviving comprehensive treatment of the subject. Quintilian's teacher, Domitius Afer, had written a treatise which apparently constituted the basis of what Quintilian says here (V,vii, 7). The regular Roman procedure in courts of law was for the pleaders to deliver their speeches first, then for the witnesses to be examined. In 52 B.C., the order of speeches and witnesses in some courts was reversed under a law of Pompey,[14] but to judge from Quintilian's remark this change was only temporary (V,vii,25). The effect of presenting the witnesses after the speeches was doubtless to make the speeches less concerned with evidence and more with general argument or character or emotions, for the pleaders did not yet know exactly what the witnesses would say, and the pleader for the prosecution sometimes tried to keep secret even the names of his expected witnesses.

Quintilian discusses examination of witnesses from the point of view both of the prosecution and the defense. Either side could employ voluntary witnesses, giving testimony in writing or in person, but the prosecutor could also have witnesses subpoenaed by the court (V,vii,1–2 and 9). As in modern courts, there was opportunity for examination and cross-examination (*interrogatio*), and Roman pleaders could even deliver a regular speech (*actio*) during examination of witnesses. Cicero's speech against Vatinius is an example.

Quintilian takes his basic rule from Afer: the orator's examination of witnesses must be based on a thorough knowledge of his case.

This will help him to prepare the court to hear the evidence in the right frame of mind, as well as to examine witnesses in person. Friendly witnesses must be carefully rehearsed so that they will be consistent and able to follow the examiner's lead. If they become confused they can be set straight by an opportune question. The pleader must beware of traps; for example, a witness who seems to be friendly but is actually sent to him by the opposition. Thus witnesses' motives for testimony must be scrutinized carefully. This precaution is especially necessary, Quintilian says, "in the case of witnesses who promise to testify what is false" (V,vii,13). Coming from Quintilian this is certainly a remarkable statement. The "good orator," it seems, may occasionally employ false witness, presumably in a just cause which cannot otherwise be defended, such as Quintilian's own case for the widow threatened with loss of her husband's estate. He also will not hesitate to imply a conspiracy, or to rail against the low birth of an opposing witness, or to frighten a timid or to mislead a foolish or to flatter a vain witness. Quintilian leaves no doubt that he wants to win, even though he disapproves of theatrical tricks. Particularly apt is his description of how to deal with a hostile witness:

In the case of a witness who is going to speak the truth only against his will, the greatest luck an examiner can have is to extract from him what he does not wish to say. This cannot be done except by means of questioning rather far from the subject. The witness will answer in a way which he thinks will not hurt the case. Subsequently, from many things which he has confessed he will be led to the point of not being able to deny what he does not wish to say. For just as in a speech we usually reach a conclusion by means of separate arguments which in themselves do not seem to tell against the defendant, then by joining them together we prove the charge, similarly a witness of this sort has to be questioned a great deal about what went before and what followed, about the scene, the occasion, the party involved, and the other matters so that he may fall into some answer which then will either force him to admit what we want or else to be inconsistent with what he has just said. (V,vii,17-18)

The rhetorical schools offered no training in cross-examinations. The student had to learn from observation and experience. The best literary models, Quintilian says, are Plato's pictures of Socrates disputing with friends and opponents.

Quintilian's account of artificial proof is divided into three parts. First are some general observations (V,viii), then discussion of the three types of proof, that based on signs (V,ix), that on arguments (V,x), and that on examples (V,xi), then remarks on how proofs are to be used (V,xiii).

Aristotle's division of artificial proof into logical, ethical, and pathetical was largely abandoned by his successors. Cicero appreciated it, but did not succeed in reestablishing it. Quintilian thinks that knowledge of the case, conveyed by rational argument, is the fundamental thing (V,viii,2–3). Presentation of the emotions, whether the gentle ones which had come to be equated with ethos, or the strong ones thought of as pathos, is at most an aid or ornament to the argument. In this discussion, he is not very interested in the common topics which had been discussed in the *Topics* of Aristotle and of Cicero, although he will shortly revert to that subject in detail. Here he lists what he calls "certain things common to all sorts of proof": questions relate to a thing or a person; arguments are drawn from consequents or opposites, from what is greater, equal, or less.

Aristotle had divided logical proof into two sorts, that based on the enthymeme and that on the example, or deduction and induction respectively. The enthymeme was defined as a rhetorical syllogism, that is, a logical argument whose premises are probabilities rather than certainties. It might or might not be formally stated in all its parts.[15] His successors, at least among the rhetoricians, rather muddied the waters by becoming very concerned about the number of parts necessary in an enthymeme. This may be seen, for example, in Cicero's early treatise *On Invention*, a typical piece of Hellenistic rhetorical theory which does, however, preserve the distinction between inductive and deductive proof and implies that the material of rhetoric is probability.[16] In the course of the first century B.C. there was a revival of interest in Aristotle, sparked by new editions of some of his works.[17] This revival may help to explain why Quintilian's account of proof seems slightly more Aristotelian than are the surviving early first century B.C. rhetorical treaties.

Quintilian states that artificial proof is dependent on signs, arguments, and examples (V,ix,1). Signs are of two sorts, depending on whether they point to a necessary or a likely conclusion. The Aristotelian distinction between certainty and probability is therefore made at the outset. Signs pointing to a certain conclusion may appear in a speech, but they allow no room for argument and thus are not parts of artificial proof. Probable signs also are in themselves often inartificial, for example bloody clothes, a shriek, a bruise, but something can be inferred from them and thus they are a part of the process of artificial proof; they are not themselves arguments, but they may be used in making arguments. The problem of classification might have been avoided if Quintilian had kept to the concept of deductive and inductive proof, and shown that signs are a material of proof, but not a process of proof as is argument or the use of example.

Once signs are disposed of, Quintilian is left with two categories which he calls argument and example, but which correspond to Aristotle's enthymeme and example. He devotes a chapter to each.

In that on argument (V,x) he begins, as he often does, with a brief historical review of the uses of relevant words, *enthymema, epicheirema, apodeixis,* and *argumentum.* His own view seems to be that the discussions have been something of a tempest in a teapot. All the words refer to pretty much the same thing and the most convenient term to use in Latin is *argumentum.* This is defined as "a reasoning setting forth a proof by which one thing is concluded from another and which confirms what is doubtful from what is not doubtful" (V,x,11). Something has to be assumed to start with: Quintilian accepts whatever is perceived by the senses, for example, things we see or hear; secondly, whatever is common opinion, for example, that the gods exist or that respect is owed to parents; in addition, whatever is provided for by law, whatever is the custom of the country where the case is being pleaded, whatever has been agreed to by the litigants, whatever has already been proved, and finally whatever the opponent does not contradict. He goes on to mention the orator's need for wide knowledge in handling arguments, something which Cicero had always stressed, and then the fact that arguments establish various degrees of probability. By this he means that certain kinds of action are more or less probable when attributed to a particular kind of person under a particular circumstance. Probability thus is connected with character *(mores),* the Aristotelian ethos (V,x,19).

From here on, almost to the end of the long chapter, Quintilian lists *loci* of arguments, taking up in detail the topics which he had mentioned very briefly in his general observations on artificial proof in chapter viii. Some of these commonplaces are substantival: arguments from persons may be drawn from their birth, country, age, education, and so on; arguments concerned with things are suggested by consideration of cause, time, place, opportunity, or the like. The student is here furnished with a checklist of topics in his search for materials of proof. Other commonplaces are formal topics, such as comparative arguments which prove the greater from the less or the less from the greater. The material here could, of course, be either persons or things. At the end, Quintilian remains dissatisfied with these topics as a system of proof, for each case is unique. The best argument is apt to come from the specific combination of circumstances of a case, and too much searching out of textbook arguments may even impede a case. Proof thus cannot be learned from books, but requires a much wider knowledge and especially practical experience (V,x,119–123).

The alternate source of artificial proof is the use of examples. This Quintilian calls "extrinsic," because the orator brings in a support for his case from some analogous external source (V,xi,1 and 36). Reasoning from examples is inductive, and according to Quintilian is best illustrated by the method of Socrates. His view here is close to that of Aristotle, for he wants to use *exemplum* to translate the Greek *paradeigma* and thus to make it the alternative to *argumentum,* by which he means Aristotle's *enthymema.* The two great techniques of induction and deduction are thus sharply distinguished; at the same time *exemplum* is in turn distinguished into historical example, *exemplum* in a narrow sense, including citations from legend as well as actual history, and *similitudo,* comparison, though all examples involve some similarity, dissimilarity, or contrariety. Deductive argument also had been said often to be comparative since it involves a reasoning from greater to lesser or lesser to greater or equal to equal, but these comparisons are not extrinsic: they involve drawing a conclusion about a man or thing on the basis of some analogous features of that man or thing: "he who has accepted money when sitting on a jury will also accept money to give false witness" (V,x,87). The comparison involved in *similitudo* is, on the other hand, between two different people or things, one outside of the case at hand: "just as those who are used to receiving something at an election are usually most hostile to those candidates whose money they think has been withheld, similarly judges of a similar sort have come to court antagonistic to the defendant" (V,xi,22). Quintilian is apparently the first ancient writer to distinguish clearly between comparison as a form of proof and comparison as an ornament of style, which he does by inserting in Book V a cross-reference to his discussion of ornament in Book VIII.[18] Comparison as a form of proof need not take any particular stylistic form, though it should avoid metaphor and be made "from things nearly equal." A comparison between two political situations, as in the example given above, is more cogent than a comparison between rather different things which may even be invalid: "as a new ship is more serviceable than an old one, so it is with friendship" (V,xi,26).

After discussing comparison, Quintilian touches briefly on an analogous matter, the citation of the opinion of others as authorities. He does not mean specific legal precedents, which are inartificial proofs, but quotations from wise men, the gods, or proverbs.

The twelfth chapter is concerned with the manner of presenting proofs. Some are strong by themselves, others in a group, others if supported. There is also here a reference to the Aristotelian categories of ethical and pathetical proof (V,xii,9), largely ignored by most Roman rhetoricians. Typically, we are told that the arrangement of arguments should be as the particular case requires, though we should not move from strongest to weakest (V,xii,14). The whole discussion of proof is then brought to an end with a bit of fancy writing in which Quintilian protests the lack of practicality and vigor in declamation. From the context it is clear that he means the avoidance of argumentation and proof which give substance to a speech and the indulgence of conceits of style and poetic effects. He had noted the tendency at the outset of his discussion of artificial proof. In this later passage a comparison is worked out between the effete eloquence of the schools and the specious beauty of a castrated slave, which Quintilian finds revolting. It is enough for him that it is unnatural. In oratory too, Quintilian says, the teacher must aim at creating a manly vigor in his pupil.[19]

After the proof, the next part of a speech, though not always needed, is the refutation of the opposing arguments, and this Quintilian surveys in chapter xiii of Book V. His remarks are generally applicable to defense speeches as a whole, which he says are difficult to manage: almost anybody can bring a charge, but only an eloquent speaker will be a successful defender. Since a defense attorney could not subpoena witnesses, and since he did not know ahead of time what arguments his opponent would use, a great deal depended on his quick-wittedness. Successes of irresponsible but ambitious informers were perhaps in the back of Quintilian's mind.

The discussion of refutation falls into two main parts: substance (V,xiii,4–14) and manner (V,xiii,15–52). The former is rather briefly handled in terms of stasis. Though that term does not occur, it is said that the fact must be denied or justified or the legal procedure challenged. Categories of stasis are also used in discussing the manner of refutation, which may consist of flat denial, or of demonstrating inconsistency or irrelevance or the like, or of mitigation of the words and values placed on something, or of attacking the opposing speaker, or of the use of humor. Several times in the course of the chapter, Quintilian warns against the artificiality of the methods used in the rhetorical schools where, he says, speakers sometimes act as though they have no opponent (V,xiii,36) or conversely try to anticipate the arguments of an imaginary opponent (V,xiii,45). Quintilian is largely opposed to anticipation of arguments, differing in this from most previous rhetoricians. His position is that in fact it rarely works well, for the second speaker can only too easily capitalize on the situation, either ridiculing the weakness of the imagined arguments, or claiming that his opponent would never have referred to them if he had not recognized their power. This seems to be one of the clearest places where Quintilian's own practical experience and observation have taught him to distrust a traditional piece of rhetorical dogma. His objections only apply to the introduction of actual arguments; he thinks a prosecutor *should* try to anticipate the defense attorney's predictable appeals to pity and to foresee the overall view of the case which the defense will take (VI,i,20).

The last chapter of Book V is a kind of appendix to the discussion of enthymeme and epicheireme in chapter x. In the first discussion, Quintilian seemed slightly impatient with these terms and did not insist on their exact use, but here he is clearer about what each is. The chapter is not foreshadowed and is slightly out of place; furthermore, the general remarks with which chapter xiii ended would make a good end to the book. Possibly Quintilian felt dissatisfied with his treatment of arguments and added chapter xiv while making revisions for publication. His view here is essentially that of Cicero and other post-Aristotelian writers: an epicheireme is a rhetorical syllogism. Both consist of three parts, proposition, assumption, and conclusion, but the epicheireme deals with probabilities, the syllogism with certainties. In his examples, Quintilian does not seem to understand very clearly what constitutes a proposition and what a conclusion (V,xiv,10). He is not a logician and his immediate sources were perhaps also confused. An enthymeme is presented as a syllogism, or presumably an epicheireme, lacking some of its parts, usually a statement with some kind of supporting clause, for example "virtue is totally good, for that only is good which no one is able to put to a bad use" (V,xiv,24–25). Despite the Aristotelian influence discernible in this book, Quintilian does not observe that epicheireme has come to be used in the sense Aristotle had given to enthymeme.

The book finally ends with a rather Ciceronian passage on the need for richness and force in oratory. A speech must not consist solely of logical arguments; it is not addressed to men of learning, but to a public that may be uneducated and must be impressed. Contemporary Greek orators make a mistake in constructing chains of arguments and avoiding ornament; a metaphor often brings much light to a subject. All of this provides a good transition to the contents of the next book. Throughout the fifth book, Quintilian is dealing with a subject which he regarded as important, but not particularly congenial. It is characteristic of him to work his way through it dutifully. In Book VI, however, he comes to the last part of a speech, the peroration, where purely oratorical rather than partly logical, qualities dominate, and where, in common with most Romans, he sees the greatest room for art.

The introduction to Book VI is the passage referred to in our first chapter, in which Quintilian describes the loss of his wife and sons. It seems likely that the passage is here because the death of his elder son happened at the time Quintilian was composing this part of the work, but the emotional tone is certainly suitable for the ensuing discussion of how to awaken the emotions. Quintilian sometimes likes to illustrate a technique at the same time that he describes it ( e.g.,IX,ii,6 ).

The primary topic of Book VI is the peroration, the one part of a speech which has not yet been examined. Quintilian takes the view that perorations have two functions; one is recapitulation and the other is emotional appeal. The former is discussed briefly ( VI,i,1–8 ), the latter extensively ( VI,i,9–55 ). Quintilian claims that the Attic orators avoided emotionalism because this was forbidden in Athenian courts, but this is certainly an overstatement. Perhaps Quintilian has over extended the rule against emotionalism before the Areopagus mentioned by Aristotle, though late in the fourth century some restriction may have been imposed against theatrical devices.[20] Emotionalism had been a strong part of oratory at Rome from the beginning, stronger indeed than logical proof, as seen for example in fragments of Cato or the Gracchi. Quintilian follows Cicero in thinking it is one of the most characteristic features of the great orator.

Emotion should not be forgotten in any part of the speech in Quintilian's view, but it figures especially in two parts, the exordium, where the emotional factors are first intimated, and the peroration, where they are fully developed. The various commonplaces are considered from the point of view of both sides: the prosecution is more apt to try to awaken feelings of outrage and horror, the defense to mitigate them or to appeal to pity. Emotions can be awakened not only by words, but by action. Quintilian does not reject theatricalities like the wearing of squalid clothes or the display of bloodstained swords and wounds, but these must be carefully handled so as not to awaken laughter, and the client must cooperate with care (VI,i, 37–43). Characteristically he prefers emotional devices which grow naturally out of the case, and dislikes artificialities like pictures meant to terrify the jury or the forced tears of children made to cry by having their ears boxed.

Though this chapter is primarily concerned with appeal to the emotions, Quintilian, on completing it, did not feel that he had dealt in adequate depth with the overall function of the orator in bending the minds of the audience; he added a second chapter dealing with the subject in a wider sense and in greater detail. Almost anybody can learn to present a decent proof, he claims, but what really demonstrates eloquence is the rare power to induce some special frame of mind in the judge and lead him to tears or anger. The orator must be at his greatest when the proofs are against him; his finest achievement is a tear in the eye of a judge. In awakening it, he performs his most characteristic function (VI,ii,7).

The discussion which follows, not a long one, has two special features. The first is the concept of ethos and pathos here advanced. The second is the technique of using images in the mind. In Aristotle, ethos and pathos, together with rational argument, are regarded as three independent means of proof. Ethos is the demonstration of character, especially the character of the speaker, who in Greece was ordinarily one of the principals in the case, not an advocate. If he can show himself to be a good man, he is helping to support his argument. Though in Aristotle's theory ethos is coordinate with argument, in fact it tends to be subsidiary to it. The same is true of pathos, which refers to the emotion a speaker is able to raise in the breasts of his audience in an attempt to stir them to a personal understanding of his plight or to determination to act.

As has already been suggested, the subsequent history of these concepts is somewhat checkered. The Hellenistic theorists lost sight of the three coordinate means of proof, and thought of emotional appeal primarily as a feature of the peroration of a speech. On the other hand, in actual oratory, especially at Rome, character and emotion played very marked roles, sometimes completely overshadowing rational argument, which was always too much like pettifoggery from the point of view of a Roman traditionalist. In *On the Orator*, Cicero revived the Aristotelian concept in the form of three duties of the orator: to teach, to charm, and to move. This is not quite the same thing, for it suggests that ethos is not so much a matter of the moral earnestness or uncorruptibility of the speaker as of affability or manners, a point which Cicero actually makes.[21]

Quintilian's view is derived from Cicero's: ethos and pathos are degrees of the same thing. He translates the former as *proprietas morum*, or good manners, the latter as *affectus* or passion ( VI,ii,9 and 20). The one makes clear the moral character of the speaker and shows his goodness and that of his client, a vestige of the Aristotelian account, but it always is gentle and mild or, at its strongest, ironic. It pervades and conciliates, while pathos commands and disturbs; thus friendship is ethos, love is pathos (VI,ii,12). Pathos is otherwise made up of strong emotions like anger, hatred, fear, envy, or pity. Ethos requires nothing elevated or sublime, but rather propriety and probability. What is called the "middle style" is suitable to it; pathos is *deinosis*, abundant overriding force, seen best in the power of Demosthenes. Quintilian presents his view of the subject as though it were commonly held, and perhaps it was, but among extant writers his account is unique.

Quintilian is a teacher. Having described pathos he must explain, if possible, how it is to be achieved. Ethos is perhaps an easier matter and thus not discussed; if the orator is a good man, as required, his goodness will find its natural expression in his manners. But pathos cannot be convincingly expressed without first being felt:

Wherefore, in those passions which we wish to be realistic, let us be like those who truly suffer from them, and let our speech flow from the state of mind which we wish to produce in the judge. Will he grieve who listens to me speaking without grief? Will he be angry if the very person who stirs and demands his anger suffers nothing of the sort? (VI,ii,27)

To produce the feelings of pathos in the orator, Quintilian outlines a technique of *visiones*, images (VI,ii,29–36). Though probably based on Greek psychology, on the known methods of writers and actors, and to some extent on suggestions of Cicero,[22] the rhetorical theory outlined in the passage is apparently chiefly a contribution of Quintilian himself. The speaker must imagine to himself all the action, all the details of whatever has happened, for example, the whole circumstances of a murder, as though he were present. Just as does an actor, he must enter into a role. Quintilian recommends that this be attempted in rhetorical schools and claims that it is the secret of his own oratorical ability. It would, of course, be especially effective in the statement of the case, the part in which he specialized.

Another kind of emotion is humor, the subject of the long third chapter of Book VI.[23] This had been studied in Greece by Theophrastus, whose account is lost, and its role in rhetoric is discussed by Cicero in a famous passage in *On the Orator*.[24] Quintilian refers to Cicero's remarks and they probably constitute his major source, though he regroups a good deal of the material and clarifies some of it. He does not begin with Cicero's fundamental distinction between *cavillatio*, or a humorous, often ironic, tone pervading an entire work, and *dicacitas*, or isolated humorous thrusts, but the concepts are embedded in his discussion. Many of his examples are taken from Cicero, but he also quotes imperial orators and especially his own witty teacher Domitius Afer. Clearly Quintilian is not very interested in theories of humor, but in how humor can be practically utilized in the courtroom, whether to dispel grave emotions prejudicial to a client or to divert attention from inconvenient facts or to refresh and interest tired judges, but he repeatedly worries about the danger of losing dignity through unsuitable humor. He thinks it might be possible to get some practice in the use of humor in themes of declamation (VI,iii,15).

With the account of humor, Quintilian has almost finished what he has to say about invention, but he adds some remarks on *altercatio*, or debate, and on judgment. Although the latter is an important aspect of Quintilian's rhetoric, the discussion (VI,v) is not a very interesting one and seems to have been included primarily to show that it had not been overlooked. The former (VI,iv), however, is unique. We know that Roman judicial process normally consisted of opening speeches by the opposing sides, then of the examination of witnesses, but there commonly seems, perhaps after the introduction of witnesses, to have been an informal debate, occasionally degenerating into a raucous argument between the two sides about points at issue. It has been suggested that in revising speeches for publication, Cicero sometimes included material from such debates, but we cannot be certain, and it is difficult to know exactly what went on.[25] Altercations were not otherwise published, and since the subject was given no attention in the rhetorical schools we do not have discussion of it in most rhetoricians. But Quintilian characteristically takes the view that he is preparing not declaimers but real orators, who must therefore be able to debate. He protests at the way some orators deliver a set speech for a client and then withdraw, turning the conduct of the trial over to inferiors: this was not supposed to be allowed in public cases (VI,iv,7). A debater must be quick-witted; he must know his case thoroughly, always a basic need to Quintilian; he must not allow emotion to blind or mislead him; he must always keep the point of the dispute clearly in mind; an eye must always be kept on the judge. The technique somewhat resembles the examination of witnesses, which was discussed earlier. Whether Quintilian had his rhetorical students practice *altercatio* is not clear; he says practice is possible and useful (VI,iv,21).

## III  *Arrangement*

At the beginning of Book VII Quintilian claims that he has said enough about invention and that the material will remain a confused heap until *dispositio*, or arrangement, orders and interrelates it. Invention and arrangement are useless without each other; this is doubtless why Book VII was grouped with Books III to VI rather than set apart in the outline of the whole work in the first preface.

Quintilian takes a more profound view of arrangement than had some other rhetoricians, though it leads him into some repetition and confusion. In classical Greek rhetorical handbooks, arrangement had meant the parts of a speech (exordium, narration, etc.); it is so viewed in the second half of the third book of Aristotle's *Rhetoric*. Hellenistic rhetoricians, however, brought these parts into discussion of invention, sometimes by means of the three kinds of oratory, considering for example the proper subjects for the proof in a judicial as compared with a deliberative speech. In the *Rhetoric to Herennius* the result is to leave little to say under the heading of arrangement, though the author does comment briefly on the order in which arguments should be stated. Quintilian has not really departed from this tradition: he discusses the parts of a speech in connection with invention, as we have seen, taking up laudatory, deliberative, and judicial oratory in turn, and he does have something to say about the order of arguments in his account of arrangement, but he adds quite a lot more, for he views arrangement as involving the whole question of the division of the subject and thus of the process of thought by which the orator brings his material into natural, coherent form (VII,x,5–9). This process involves the discovery of the stasis of the case, and thus after an introductory chapter Quintilian is led to take up each kind of stasis in turn, primarily to show the logical division each entails and thus how the speech is to be arranged (e.g., VII,iv,19), but in fact in many passages the element of arrangement is not very conspicuous, for Quintilian becomes interested in stasis as such, though of course he had already treated the subject in Book III. From a purely educational point of view he perhaps thought this double treatment justified: he viewed an understanding of stasis as essential and as rather difficult. In order to grasp it, the student must be repeatedly brought back to it. A treatment of arrangement which did not take into account the different requirements of the various categories of stasis might fairly be criticized as superficial.

The seventh book is thus a characteristic part of Quintilian's work. It has the consistent viewpoint of the teacher trying to show the novice how to proceed—"I shall always think of students as though they were my own," he remarks (VII,iii,30). It shows also Quintilian's fundamental belief in proceeding according to nature. A very interesting passage describes the train of thought which he himself used in deciding how to manage a case (VII,i,23–28).[26] The order of the questions which the orator asks himself will not be the order in which he will speak: the former moves from the particular to the general; the latter, a natural order as Quintilian conceives it, moves from the general to the particular. Thus, what comes to mind first ought often to be spoken last; for example, speaking against a hero who is offered anything he chooses as a reward, a declaimer might raise the objection, "You ought not to choose another man's wife." But though this may be what he first thinks, he ought not to be content with it and should seek what stands beyond it, which would be the more general objection, "you ought not to take anything that is private property." Then the final step backwards is to say that which is the first conclusion from the general heading, "you should choose nothing inequitable." Having reasoned backward this way, the orator can reverse the steps and speak in accordance with nature, moving from general to particular: the hero ought not to choose anything inequitable; more specifically he ought not to choose private property, and in particular he ought not to choose another man's wife. Only when the proposition is grasped can the orator decide what is the natural thing to be said first (VII,i,26).

Even difficult questions can be dealt with by an orator of moderate ability if he is content to follow nature as his leader and does not give all of his attention to a showy style, and an example of a complicated declamation is cited to show how this is true. It is nature that teaches us to appeal from the words to the intention of a law, and indeed, the whole stasis system is an example of natural order, since the first question naturally is whether an action took place at all, then whether the action is correctly defined as a crime, and thirdly whether the action has some quality which can justify it (VII,i,66). Should the orator deal first with the person who performs an action or with the motive which leads him to act? Cicero preferred to treat motives first, but Quintilian thinks it is most natural to begin with the person: it is a more general question to ask whether he can be imagined to have committed a criminal act of any sort than to ask whether he had motive for this particular criminal action (VII, ii,39).

## IV  *Style*

The preface to Book VIII makes it clear that a new major division of the work begins at this point, the discussion of style, which extends well into Book XI. A sign of a fresh start is that in this preface the content of the previous books is recapitulated. Important as are the subjects already discussed, they cannot in Quintilian's view make a man eloquent: this is chiefly a matter of the expression of what he has thought, and thus of style. On the other hand, to regard style as something independent of subject is to corrupt it. Quintilian seeks a healthy style, by which he means one in conformity with nature, shunning cosmetics and feminine adornment and seeking masculine strength of directness. If a man understands the nature of speaking, he will collect from his reading a useful supply of words; he will know how to arrange them; by exercise he will strengthen his ability until it is ready for his use. He must not fear to lose a word; he must do nothing solely for the sake of a word. The speech he achieves must have its charm not from some kind of unnatural deformity, but from the honor and dignity which attend it.

The basic structure which Quintilian follows is a consideration of certain qualities of style. These are first stated in Book VIII,*pr.*,31, where we are told that words should be good Latin, clear *(significantia)*, ornamented, well placed. Subsequently (VIII,i,1) style is divided into matters involving words individually and words in context. The former must be good Latin, clear *(perspicua,* this time), ornamented, and suited to what we wish to accomplish. Words in context should be *emendata,* or correctly inflected, properly formed, and figured. In the course of the following books Quintilian discusses correctness, clarity, and ornamentation, including the arrangement of words, while much later (XI,i) he treats the more subjective and general matter of the appropriate *(apte)* use of style. His system is thus a rather free adaptation of the so-called virtues of style; indeed he uses the word *virtutem* of propriety (XI,i,1). We know these "virtues" best from Cicero's *On the Orator,* where it is said that the orator must speak in good Latin, clearly, with ornamentation, and suitably to the subject,[27] and there can be no doubt that Quintilian derived them from Cicero, but he also probably found them discussed in later writers like Celsus.

Although the various qualities involved are touched upon in the third book of Aristotle's *Rhetoric,* to judge from Cicero's references it was Theophrastus who first systematically discussed the "virtues" in his famous lost treatise *On Style.*[28] In Hellenistic times there was some development: the Stoics, for example, tried to add the virtue of brevity, and the list of figures of speech was continually enlarged as a part of ornamentation. Propriety lost ground, probably because it lacked any specific precepts or categories: it has almost disappeared in the version of the *Rhetoric to Herennius.* Quintilian points out that Cicero treats the subject in a single sentence (XI,i,4).

In outline, Quintilian's account of style is based on Cicero's, but it is longer, partly from his own elaboration, partly because he incorporates considerable specific material which had been discussed by rhetoricians of the early empire. In keeping with his general approach he has further expanded the subject to include some other topics which are relevant but had usually been discussed separately, for example how to acquire word power from reading or how to apply the principle of imitation. In adding these topics, Quintilian shows again that his concern is educational: how to teach a man to speak, not how to analyze the stylistic devices of an extant speech.

Most rhetoricians agreed that correctness and clarity are essential to good style, but they increasingly devoted their attention to ornament. This is true, for example, of Cicero's account in *On the Orator.* Correctness might be logically regarded as the field of the grammarian, and Quintilian makes a cross-reference to his discussion of grammar in Book I, adding only that language should not be alien or foreign, and the famous remark, "Asinius Pollio even thought that there was some kind of Paduan quality in Titus Livy, a man of wonderful eloquence" (VIII,i,3). Clarity is given slightly more attention, divided into consideration of the use of words in their proper sense[29] and the fault of obscurity, which arises not only from faulty diction, but from over-extended sentences, exaggeration, parenthesis, grammatical ambiguity, and redundancy, or conversely from excessive brevity and the like. Clarity is especially important for an orator: we must take care not only that the judge "can understand, but can under no circumstances *fail* to understand" (VIII,ii,24).

The account of ornamentation then begins in chapter iii of Book VIII and continues through the end of Book IX. What Quintilian aims at is of course not some kind of padding or incidental decoration, least of all the soft decadence of style against which he repeatedly protests. To the Roman ear the word "ornament" suggests distinction and excellence, the possession of resources ready for any challenge; it is a vital and useful quality which Quintilian says contributes first of all to the fame of the orator: "in other aspects of rhetoric the orator is seeking to gain the approval of the learned; in this he seeks popular praise; he fights not only with showy, but even with flashing arms" (VIII,iii,2). The quality in turn aids the orator's practical purpose, for by it he compels attention and bends the audience to his will. Ornament is thus to style what emotion is to proof. Naturally it will vary greatly in quality and quantity with the requirements of the particular speech, and like all qualities of style it may exist in individual words or in words in context. These two topics are discussed in turn, first individual words (VIII,iii, 24–39).

Quintilian divides words into three kinds: proper (including both common and archaic words), newly coined words, and metaphors. The suitability of archaic diction was debated for centuries at Rome; Cicero limited it largely to poetry;[30] Sallust in the first century B.C. and Fronto in the second century A.D. were notable proponents. Quintilian's position could be predicted by anyone who knows him: archaic words can have great charm when used in moderation, but affected use must be avoided. No rules are laid down to distinguish right usage from wrong, but examples are given, and the taste of Virgil praised. Quintilian of course does not mean to canonize Virgilian vocabulary, much of which he would have thought unsuitable in prose. In theory he can see no objection to word coinage, for words now old once were new and the process is thus a natural one. In fact, however, coinages often sounded harsh to him, and he would limit the orator's coinage to new derivatives and compounds (VIII, iii,36). The third category of diction, metaphor, is not discussed here but postponed to a later point since a metaphor, though it may be a single word, cannot be satisfactorily identified as a metaphor except in some context.

The heart of the subject of style is ornamentation in connected discourse. To Quintilian it involves two stages; he calls the first the choice of style or expression, the second the choice of the means of expression (VIII,iii,40). In the first he includes matters of stress, manner, tone, length, and mood, in other words the choice of the proper kind of style for the subject. Second comes the choice of the particular devices to be used to attain the desired style, including metaphor, figures, epigram, and word arrangement. This interesting division of the subject, which suggests questions of appropriateness and the psychological effect of various devices, is not systematically carried out, though something is said on some of the topics of the first stage, and the devices of the second stage are subsequently all discussed. Here an examination of faults of style is first inserted, and a different division of the subject of ornament then advanced (VIII,iii,61). The text of this second division is corrupt, but it is fortunately clearly referred to in what follows (VIII,iii,62 and 86) and can be reconstructed. Quintilian apparently said: "Ornament is something more than what is intelligible [*perspicuus*] and probable. Its first [two] steps consist in expressing what you wish to say lucidly [*clare*] and vividly [*evidenter*]; the third step, which is properly called polish [*cultus*] gives greater brilliance [*nitidiora*]." [31] In what follows Quintilian takes the first two steps together to distinguish four different sources of clarity and vividness: first, representation, which can be a matter of getting vividness by a completely detailed description or by mentioning attendant "accidents," the shuddering of fear, for example; second, the use of similes; third, pregnant brevity; and fourth, what is called "emphasis," a deliberate choice of a suggestive word. Characteristically, Quintilian urges following nature; vivid representation is not difficult if we describe what is really there (VIII,iii,71). Some similes and emphasis are a normal part of everyday language (VIII,iii,81 and 86).

But lucidity and vividness are not enough. An additional step toward ornamentation must be taken and other qualities added to achieve a really great style (VIII,iii,86). A number of qualities are mentioned which had been discussed by Greek rhetoricians, but what Quintilian mainly has in mind are devices of amplification, tropes, figures, and rhythmical composition, which he takes up from here through the end of Book IX. Amplification and its opposite are discussed first (VIII,iv). The different types are all matters of amplifying the thought to make it seem more important and more emphatic; they are not simply ways to say something at greater or lesser length. Next, chapter v on *sententiae,* or aphorisms, is inserted. Quintilian thinks his readers will expect it since *sententiae,* or aphorisms, particularly in the form of epigrammatic climaxes to paragraphs, were much sought in the first century A.D. His view here is typical of his attitude toward style: brilliant *sententiae* can be very effective in moving a judge or winning admiration for a speaker, but a speech made up of *sententia* after *sententia,* as declamations sometimes were, is tiresome and defeats its own purpose. In such a speech some of the *sententiae* will almost certainly be absurd through constant striving for cleverness; none will stand out clearly if all the speech is epigrammatic; and the whole will be jerky and affected, sacrificing coherence and unity to immediate applause.

Chapter vi, on tropes, is an important but particularly unsatisfactory chapter. Quintilian defines a trope as the change, with artistic result, of a word or group of words from its literal meaning to another (VIII,vi,1). Although he dismisses the various *genera* and *species* as a matter for grammarians, he recognizes two major groups, those involving an enlargement of the meaning of a passage as well as its ornamentation, and those used only for the sake of ornament and amplification, or we might say for decoration and emphasis. His initial definition only fits the first group, and when he discusses tropes in the next book he revises the definition to include all substitution of a word or words for others, and changes in word order as well (IX,i,4–6). Throughout the discussion of tropes Quintilian is at pains to identify both Greek and Latin terms and to determine the suitability for prose of what are basically poetic devices. The original definition, of course, well fits a metaphor, but Quintilian wants to use that term of only one type of trope. He defines metaphor as the transference of a noun (with which he would include an adjective as his examples show) or verb "from the place in which it belongs to a place where an exact word is lacking or a transferred word is better than the literal word" (VIII,vi,5–6). He has in mind a relatively simple exchange of analogous words in which the effect is to move the feelings, to stamp something with a special meaning, and to place things vividly before the eyes (VIII,vi,19). He follows Cicero in calling metaphor a short form of comparison rather than regarding metaphor as the larger category as does Aristotle.[32] As is the case with other ancient critics, he does not have a clear conception of what today we call a simile.[33]

After discussing metaphor, Quintilian turns to other tropes, all of which could be regarded as special forms of metaphor, though he does not point out that fact. These other tropes, he claims, do not have all the effects of metaphor, but give variety to the language, thus somewhat enlarging the meaning. The tropes mentioned are synecdoche (VIII,vi,19–22), which is use of the whole for a part, or genus for species, or effect for cause, or the opposite, for example *mucro* ("point") or *ferrum* ("steel") for a sword; then metonymy (VIII,vi,23–28), which is the use of a proper name for an object: "Ceres" for grain or "Virgil" for Virgil's poems. It also includes the use of adjectives transferred from effect to cause, as when death is called "pale," or old age "sad," the rationale being the personification involved. Antonomasia (VIII,vi,29–30) is the opposite of metonymy, the substitution of an epithet or description for a proper name. Onomatopoiia, or word coinage (VIII,vi,31–33), is also a trope, but only allowable for an orator in the coining of derivatives. Quintilian is slightly more negative about it here than in chapter iii. Catachresis (VIII,vi,34–36) is the use of the nearest available term when an exact one is lacking, as for example *acetabula* is properly a vinegar flask, but is used of other flasks which have no name of their own. There is some inconsistency between the discussion of the use of a metaphor when no exact term is available (VIII,vi,5–6) and the claim that we must distinguish catachresis from metaphor (VIII,vi, 35). In the latter passage Quintilian is thinking of metaphor in a narrower sense. The final trope involving alteration of meaning is metalepsis (VIII,vi,37–39), which is a kind of word play, and not much recommended. For example, *canto* can mean either "sing" or "repeat" and thus could be used metaphorically for either *cano* ("sing") or *dico* ("say"). It is metalepsis if another step is taken and *cano* ("sing") is used for *dico* ("say").

All of these tropes seem to be basically metaphorical. The tropes which follow, Quintilian says (VIII,vi,40), are used not for the sake of the meaning but for ornament. He discusses epithet, various kinds of allegory, periphrasis, hyperbaton, and hyperbole. There are many problems here, especially involving hyperbaton, or artificial word order (VIII,vi,62–67). It hardly belongs with the other tropes and leads Quintilian into the inconsistency of saying first that it is used for the sake of ornament (VIII,vi,65), and then a few lines later claiming that unless the meaning is affected it is not a trope at all (VIII,vi,67). Most of these tropes may involve metaphor, indeed it is in connection with allegory that we are told for perhaps the first time in history that we must not mix our metaphors (VIII,vi,50), but all this group can occur without metaphor, in which case Quintilian regards them simply as ornaments. It is easier to see this in the case of epithet, where amplification and decoration are secured by adding a word or phrase, or in the case of periphrasis, where some roundabout phrase is substituted, but it might be truly insisted that the meaning can be made more exact by these devices. "Night" in fact means rather different things: a time of darkness, a time of rest, a time for secrecy, a time for love. When Virgil says, "it was the time when the first quiet begins for weary mortals and quite pleasingly coils upon them as a gift of the gods," he has said something more than "it was night," and the passage has considerable significance for Dido's situation. Quintilian however says that the passage is a periphrasis, and used for ornamentation alone (VIII,vi,60). On the other hand, he says that *vertex* when used of the "brow" of a hill is a metaphor, and thus is used for the sake of meaning, but in fact the metaphor is trite and has relatively no significance in the passage he quotes (VIII,vi,10). Similar criticism could be made of other examples.

The end result is that Quintilian's discussion of tropes seems rather unsatisfactory. The initial definition is inadequate. The categories are arbitrary and ill-arranged; particularly, the relation of metaphor to the other tropes is not adequately explained; hyperbaton hardly belongs here at all and would be better treated under composition in Book IX. Finally, the illustrative examples have been rather superficially examined. This is true in general of Quintilian's discussion of style. He was not himself a very good stylist; indeed, his own use of metaphor is often singularly stiff, as seen for example in the nautical images at the beginning of Book XII and elsewhere. One reason why he does not handle tropes well is perhaps the fact that he was accustomed to think of them as more poetic than oratorical and thus the business of grammarians, another is his lack of sympathy for any technical terms.

The first three chapters of Book IX make up Quintilian's long account of figures of speech, a subject of great interest to rhetoricians of the empire. Unfortunately, our knowledge of the history of the subject is somewhat fragmentary. Probably the experiments in style of the Greek orator Gorgias in the fifth century B.C. suggested giving names to certain devices of word arrangement, sound effect, or expression of thought. During the Hellenistic period the list was expanded and a general distinction between figures of thought and figures of diction was recognized. By the late second century B.C., the study of figures was being applied to Latin as well as Greek, though for a long time Latin terminology was not standardized. Thus the Greek word for figure, *schema*, is translated as *ornatio* by the author of the *Rhetoric to Herennius*, as *lumen* by Cicero. In fact, Quintilian is the earliest extant writer to use *figura*, though Celsus and others had probably done so earlier in the first century A.D.[34]

In the late first century B.C. a controversy arose over the number and nature of figures (IX,i,10–14). All language takes some form; therefore it might be argued that all language is figured. Quintilian does not identify the chief propounder of this view: something close to it appears in Dionysius.[35] He indicates that it was combated by Apollodorus and Caecilius. Caecilius apparently believed in a natural language. Any departure from this constituted a figure, and he catalogued, illustrated, and perhaps arranged in groups a very considerable number of figures.[36]

Quintilian does not appear to follow any one earlier writer, though he mentions several including Cicero and Caecilius. Possibly there is more influence of Caecilius than we can detect from our limited knowledge of what he said. Certainly Quintilian's basic view is that of Caecilius, though he has rephrased it to avoid the suggestion that there is anything unnatural about figures. His position is that the word has two meanings (IX,i,10). On the one hand it can be loosely applied to any configuration of language, but this is not very useful and the proper meaning is an intentional departure from the ordinary and simple form of thought or expression (IX,i,4 and 14). A distinction is drawn between the transference of words, either by substitution of one for another or by changes in order, which constitutes a trope, and a change in the conformation of the thought or form of the word themselves, which constitutes a figure, though Quintilian is willing to admit that there are borderline cases and cases in which both processes occur (IX,i,9, see also IX,i,16). In fact the distinction is not very valuable, for the classifications are often arbitrary and a lot less useful than a simple knowledge of possible devices and their effect.

Quintilian's admiration for Cicero's discussion of figures might have seemed strange to his own contemporaries, since Cicero's accounts in *On the Orator* and *The Orator* are both relatively short and were out of date, and some of what Quintilian wants to see in Cicero could be found in more recent authors. But Cicero has a special holiness in Quintilian's eyes; he wants to encourage others to read him, and he stresses the validity of the Ciceronian tradition. Sometimes he has to disagree with Cicero, and that is the case here, but he manages to suggest that there has been a kind of scholarly progress. Cicero's views in *The Orator* are refinements of his views in *On the Orator*, and he himself has only taken a further step.[37] This rather overstates the situation, but it is what Quintilian would like to have believed. He quotes verbatim the account of figures from both of Cicero's treatises. These are the longest quotations in the *Institutio*. They are justified by piety, for Cicero's works were easily available, though there is an increasing tendency to quote rather than simply to refer on the part of Roman writers of the empire. Readers were known to be lazy. Quintilian presents Cicero as taking slightly too wide a view of the subject and including all ornaments of style, not just figures, but Cicero will still be a valuable guide for the student. In fact, Quintilian follows the arrangement of *On the Orator*, which is reversed in *The Orator*. He prefers what he calls the "natural" order of discussing first figures of thought, then of diction (IX,i,19). Within these two categories Quintilian has made explicit groupings which are implied in Cicero's writings, but not pointed out. Finally, the function or effect associated with particular figures sometimes follows Cicero's suggestions. It is characteristic of the more careful accounts of figures in antiquity, those in the *Rhetoric to Herennius* or in *On Sublimity*, for example, that they try to perceive the psychological effect of figures, rather than simply draw up lists. Unfortunately we do not know how much psychology or what groupings appeared in Caecilius' account.

Quintilian stresses the practical utility of figures: they make arguments believable; they steal secretly into the mind of the judge; they excite emotion; they win favor for the speaker and for his cause, while avoiding monotony and social or political indiscretions from too frank language (IX,i,19–21). When he turns to examine specific figures of thought, he arranges them in three groups according to the effect they produce. First (IX,ii,6–25) are those which make proof sharper and more forceful, among which are various forms of question and answer or anticipation. Cicero too had discussed these as a group. Second, and considerably more numerous (IX,ii,26–96), are figures which intensify emotions, which Quintilian earlier identified with pathos or the milder emotions of ethos. Prosopopoiia and ethopoiia respectively are examples. The relationship between figures of thought and invention is thus carried on. Inserted here (IX,ii,65–95) is a discussion of figured *controversiae*, or themes in which the speaker has some hidden meaning, much beloved by the clever declaimers of the first century A.D. Finally (IX,ii,96–101), there are said to be figures of thought aiming not at proof or at emotion, but at elegance. The discussion is brief, and the figures cited are similar to those already discussed, but their purpose is ornamentation, and Quintilian seems to regard them as rather trivial. The chapter ends with a list of devices called figures of thought by earlier rhetoricians, but not accepted by Quintilian.

In chapter iii figures of diction are discussed. Initially Quintilian says there are two kinds, the grammatical, in which the form of the word creates the figure, and the rhetorical, in which the position of the word is the primary factor, and he begins with examination of the first kind: use of masculine for feminine, passive for active, comparative for positive, and the like. These would be grammatical mistakes, were it not that they are made deliberately and have some precedent or conform to some pattern. Indeed, Quintilian believes that what constitutes a figure changes in the course of time with changes in usage (IX,iii,1). As long as figures of diction are not excessive, the result is a charming variety of language which keeps alive the attention of the audience (IX,iii,27). This variety, of course, indirectly contributes to persuasion since the audience must be attentive and pleased by the speaker in order to be convinced of what he says.

Figures of the second group, the rhetorical ones, confer charm and vigor on the very thought of the passage and thus make a greater contribution (IX,iii,28). Typical are various devices of repeating or omitting words. Unexpectedly a third kind of figure is introduced, which attracts attention by appealing to the ear (IX,iii, 66–86). These are the so-called Gorgianic figures. They constitute a group certainly, but should have been presented as a subdivision of the rhetorical kind rather than an independent third category. The chapter ends, as did the previous one, with a list of devices wrongly labeled figures by others, to which is then added a brief warning against over indulgence in figures of any sort.

Quintilian's account of figures compares favorably with other ancient discussions. Over a hundred slightly differing devices are arranged, named, and adequately illustrated from writings of Cicero, Virgil, and other writers. He is not overly rigid and recognizes that a figure like irony may have differing classifications and effects, and his recommendation is always for restraint and control. It might be argued that the needs of students would be better served if instead of drawing up a list of figures he had considered the various tones or moods which a speaker might wish to create and had shown what figures contribute to that end. But Quintilian's approach is possibly the only realistic one. Particular figures really do not have particular psychological effects out of context; they intensify the thought or the emotion or give variety, and what is successful in one context will fail in another. Students are here given a wide variety of devices from which to choose, and are also given some indication of the particular effects which these figures can have in particular contexts. Taste they must develop themselves.

When first organizing his account of the ornaments of style in the third chapter of Book VIII, Quintilian had suggested the need to examine composition, and it is that topic which constitutes the lengthy final chapter of Book IX. Traditionally two related matters of arrangement had come to constitute what was known as "composition." One of these was sentence structure, the other prose rhythm. Quintilian has dealt already with some aspects of sentence structure, antithesis for example, in the chapter on figures of diction.

Both structure and rhythm had been discussed as early as the fourth century B.C. by Isocrates and Aristotle, but the most extensive treatments came in the first century B.C. from Cicero in *The Orator* and from Dionysius of Halicarnassus in his treatise *On the Arrangement of Words*. The latter's contribution is primarily to the understanding of euphony in Greek and is not mentioned by Quintilian, though he is elsewhere familiar with Dionysius' writings. Cicero's interest was primarily prose rhythm. Latin orators of the second century B.C. had begun to show some rhythmical awareness, but Cicero was the first Roman to make extensive use of prose rhythm and the first to discuss the subject in detail. The extreme Atticists, against whom he argues in *The Orator*, had not shared his enthusiasm. Cicero is Quintilian's primary inspiration here, but he announces that he will not always agree with Cicero on particular points (IX,iv,1–2).

Since nature constitutes such an important principle in Quintilian's rhetorical theory, he feels that he must begin by refuting those who regard a concern with composition as unnatural and effeminate (IX, iv,2–18). His answer is in several parts: the same objection could be made against all features of rhetorical theory, including something as basic as the conventional divisions of a speech; if allowed, it would come to the absurd extreme of destroying all artistic oratory. Secondly, progress is in itself natural and "that is most natural which nature allows to achieve the best form" (IX,iv,5). Nor should structure be regarded as necessarily effeminate, for it can give strength as well as softness. This leads to a brief discussion of the power of rhythm and music, to the conclusion that it is natural to seek rhythm, and to the assertion that even the earliest orators did so, though perhaps not in quite the same form as is now approved.

Although Quintilian's interest is primarily in rhythm, he follows the traditional arrangement of the subject, which is at least as old as Aristotle, and distinguishes first between the running style, which he says is especially suited to dialogues and letters and some minor court cases and which lacks tight cohesion between the parts, and the periodic style, made up of interrelated phrases or clauses (IX,iv, 19–21). The distinction is really more applicable to Greek prose than to Latin. According to Quintilian, either of these styles, to be artistic, must have three qualities: order, connection, and rhythm (IX,iv,22). Whether original with Quintilian or not, this seems a development and improvement over Cicero's basic divisions.[38] In discussing "order" Quintilian stresses the end of the sentence, which should rise and grow as it proceeds; the last word is frequently the most emphatic. In "connection" the traditional topic was hiatus, which Quintilian says is "not an enormous crime" (IX,iv,35). Elision will sometimes make for smoothness, but hiatus can make a passage seem fuller and suggests, as Cicero had said, that the orator is more concerned with subject than style (IX,iv,37).

Although all prose has rhythms of some sort, and good stylists in all languages choose or avoid certain patterns, no modern literature has given such emphasis to the use of suitable rhythms as did Greek and Latin. One reason probably is that in both these languages the quantity of syllables was very clearly marked and any succession of spoken words immediately presented to the ear a pattern of long and short syllables, quite independent of stress or pitch. Furthermore, Latin word order is very flexible and can easily be manipulated to achieve rhythmical effects. Another significant fact is that all ancient literature was intended to be spoken or read aloud, and the ears of speakers and hearers had become highly sensitive to the various possible effects. To a modern student not attuned to spoken Latin, the whole subject is a difficult one. It has, however, been studied in detail, and various highly refined systems of analysis have been built up, based both on the theoretical accounts of authors like Cicero and the actual practice of writers of all sorts.[39] Here we need only examine Quintilian's system and its relation to his own practice.

Like most authors Quintilian draws a distinction between rhythm and meter. Prose as a whole should be rhythmical, but not metrical. It will be rhythmical if a proportion between short and long feet

## ERRATA

Through an error of the publisher for which the author is in no way responsible the indication of short syllables was omitted on pages 91, 92, and 93 of the first printing of this book.

p. 137, for Fabius Julius read Fabius Justus.

is maintained without creating a succession of metrical feet which would characterize poetic verses. For overall rhythmical purposes the order of long and short syllables is not important, only their proportion (IX,iv,47–48). Thus the rhythm is said to be dactylic if one long syllable generally balances two short syllables, whether occurring as dactyls or as anapaests. A rhythmical pattern has no necessary length: a sentence might begin in a generally paeonic rhythm (long syllables balanced by three short syllables), move over to a dactylic rhythm, and end in a choreic rhythm of one long to one short, though in fact few sentences ever follow so clear a pattern, and Quintilian's picture of overall rhythm is too simplified. He is certainly correct, however, in saying that the more short syllables, the more rapid and hurried the effect, the more long syllables, the slower and heavier the effect (IX,iv,83). A passage is thus badly composed if the metrical effect is unsuited to the thought; it is also apparently unrhythmical if either long or short syllables so preponderate that no proportion can be felt (IX,iv,66), for the spondee (– –), the molossus (– – –), the pyrrhic (      ), and what Quintilian calls the trochee, more often known as the tribrach (      ), are not recognized as legitimate rhythms, although they will subsequently be admitted as clausulae. This does not mean that they cannot be used in combination or substitution with other feet, but they do not themselves constitute satisfactory rhythms. Rhythm is important enough, Quintilian feels, to justify giving the orator some latitude in the arrangement of his words, or in the addition or omission of words, or in the choice of alternative grammatical forms (IX,iv,58–59).

Although the overall maintenance of rhythm is important, rhythms are conspicuous at the beginnings of sentences and especially so at the ends. The rhythmical end of a sentence is called a clausula. As Quintilian puts it, the pause which follows the sentence imposes a natural limit and gives the ear an opportunity to consider what it has just heard (IX,iv,61). Clausulae are analyzed in terms of metrical feet. Quintilian wants to restrict the feet to be examined to the twelve possible combinations of two or three syllables, but he subsequently does admit the double choree (–     –     ) and the two kinds of paean (–         ,         –), all three of considerable importance in the history of rhetoric (IX,iv,79 and 95).

In describing a clausula by Quintilian's system, as in Cicero's,[40] it is never necessary to consider more than the last three feet, and if the last two can be classified as feet of three or four syllables it is only necessary to consider two. Thus the last six to eight syllables of a sentence constitute the clausula. Quintilian is aware that it is often possible to divide a succession of syllables into feet in more than one way, but he does not regard this as very important since the rhythm is the same whatever the names applied to it. In practice, his divisions in doubtful cases tend to conform to word divisions.[41] Pauses between words strengthen the rhythm, and a long word at the end of a sentence consisting of two whole feet is not, as a modern reader might have guessed, imposing, but effeminate (IX,iv,97). The role of stressed syllables in rhythm, though perhaps of some importance in practice, is ignored in theory. Other writers on rhythm, including Cicero,[42] usually regarded the last syllable of a sentence as conventionally long, for even if short by nature it was thought to be lengthened by the following pause, but Quintilian objects that even if that is true, the effect of – and – – at the end of a sentence is quite different: one is much heavier than the other (IX,iv,93). This is original and sensible, though in his analysis Quintilian does not consistently differentiate such clausulae (IX,iv,107). In a few other ways also his system differs from conventional analyses of rhythms: he does not make any provision for metrical substitutions in clausulae; thus – is not regarded as a resolution of – –, or as having any special similarity to it. Secondly, though this is less clear, Quintilian thinks elision should not be assumed in all cases where vowels come together. Apparently each passage must be judged on the basis of the effect which elision or hiatus will have on the rhythm and perhaps on the sense.[43]

Like other rhetoricians, Quintilian discusses particular combinations of feet which he regards as suitable clausulae. His basic view is that all feet will find some use in prose and that predominantly long syllables are generally apt to be more suitable than short, but he does praise certain combinations and criticize others. He agrees with other writers that a combination which constitutes the end of a line of verse is bad at the end of a prose sentence, but the beginning of a line of verse is an acceptable clausula (IX,iv,72). The traditional paeon ( –), approved by Aristotle as the ideal prose measure, but less admired by Cicero,[44] and indeed less suited to Latin than to Greek, Quintilian does not really like at all, but he hesitates to reject it totally (IX,iv,110). Endings in cretics (– –) are approved (IX,iv,107), and in a spondee preceeded by a cretic (IX,iv,97). The double choree, always identified with the flamboyant Hellenistic prose called Asianism, seems acceptable (IX,iv,103), as

are the spondee plus the iamb (– –    –) (IX,iv,99), the double bac-
chius (  – –    – –) (IX,iv,102), and a few other measures. In
general, Quintilian follows Cicero's preferences.[45]

The meters which Quintilian himself employs, like those of most
Latin writers, have been studied,[46] though the results necessarily
vary with the approach to hiatus or division taken in specific cases.
There is also variation in different parts of the work depending, presumably, on the degree of polish given to a passage or the speed or
weight desired, so that flat percentages are deceiving. Quintilian
certainly uses long syllables for weight, an example being a somber
clausula from the preface to Book XII—"per omnis difficultates
animo me sustentavi" (  – – –    – – –     – – – – – –, "I have sus-
tained myself in mind through all difficulties")—where the number
of long syllables exceeds anything he recommends. Of the clausulae
which Quintilian approves in theory, he turns out to be fond in
practice of double chorees, which constitute around twenty percent
of his clausulae, and of double cretics, which make up around eight
percent. Spondees preceded by cretics are almost as common. His
other favorite clausula, just about as common as the double cretic,
is the cretic plus choree (–  / –  ), a combination which he never
specifically recommends. It is very common in most Latin authors;
Cicero often uses it without recommending it either, but Cicero
viewed the last syllable of a sentence as long, and both he and Quintilian approve of cretic plus spondee. Possibly Quintilian's ear failed
him here; possibly he regarded the clausula as colorless and common;
most likely he simply overlooked it because Cicero, who is his major
source, had not mentioned it.

Too great emphasis on clausulae might lead to a very artificial
style. In the rest of his chapter on composition, Quintilian tries to
counteract this by taking a wider view, as usual attuned to the educational process. Students must not be overanxious about obtaining
certain rhythmical effects, he says, but must try to develop a good
ear for rhythm. If they are careful in exercises, they can eventually
speak extemporaneously in rhythmical prose. The orator must understand what kind of composition is appropriate, which in turn involves
two different matters: the construction of periods and the rhythmical
flow of a passage, a subject on which he had already said something.

On periodicity Quintilian does not have very much to say, and as
usual chiefly follows Cicero, though he slightly differs from Cicero's
definition of a colon and slightly misquotes Cicero's limitation of
the size of a period to a single breath (IX,iv,123–125).[47] A period

*(circuitus)*, he thinks, may be simply a statement with grammatical and rhythmical fullness, or it may be a statement made up of two or more parts *(membra,* Greek *cola)* which are rhythmically full, but grammatically incomplete. A phrase both rhythmically and grammatically incomplete is an *incisum (comma)* and may also constitute part of a period. A mixture of *incisa* and *membra* makes for force, a succession of *membra* for smoothness (IX,iv,126–27). The account as a whole fails to deal with the subtleties of sentence structure in Latin, or even to explain adequately what is meant by the traditional demand that a period be "rounded" at the close, but this was perhaps generally understood by readers.

The discussion of rhythmic flow (IX,iv,130–47) resumes the matter of the effect of long and short syllables in a passage and considers briefly what is appropriate in various parts of an oration, concluding with another word of warning against too much attention to rhythm rather in the spirit of Domitius Afer, Quintilian's teacher, who had harshened his cadences. The chapter as a whole seems rather informally written since some subjects are discussed twice, some in detail, some points are totally overlooked, others treated very briefly. Like all of Quintilian's discussion of style, the objective is an appropriate and useful control of language, avoiding excessive mannerism, but capable of attaining power or richness.

With the end of Book IX, the discussion of ornamentation, the third of the four virtues of style, begun in the third chapter of Book VIII, finally comes to an end. The fourth virtue of style, appropriateness or propriety, is considered in the first chapter of Book XI, though it had been repeatedly touched upon before. In between, comes the tenth book, which can best be dealt with in a separate chapter, not that it is logically a digression—the study and imitation of literary models and practice in writing and speaking are primarily thought of in connection with style, and especially in connection with the ornaments of style—but the book, however significant, is an enlargement of the ordinary plan of a rhetorical treatise, and it will be more convenient, before looking at it, to complete our examination of Quintilian's treatment of the traditional material of rhetoric.

In the introductory sections of the chapter on appropriateness, Quintilian takes his keynote once again from Cicero, who had specified that the style should be appropriate to the case, to the audience, to the speaker, and to the situation.[48] In what follows, Quintilian somewhat enlarges this list. His account is an interesting one since it brings out some of the aspects of rhetoric which most concerned him, though in a sense the topic is hopeless. How can a teacher specify what is going to be appropriate in every speech? He can, however, warn the student against specific dangers, and by pointing out some good examples and by urging moderation hope to develop a sense of taste. And this is what Quintilian does. Nominally, the chapter is a subdivision of the account of style, but it leads over into invention, as Quintilian points out (XI,1,7). In fact, appropriateness is a consideration in the use of any rhetorical technique including arguments, emotional appeals, arrangement, figures and rhythms, and delivery. Most of the chapter is not concerned with style in the narrow sense of diction and composition, but with something which might be called "tone," but had no Latin term, and in some sections the subject is specifically the propriety of the argumentation.

Quintilian's discussion is more extensive than anything in Cicero, though based on his views and largely drawing its examples from his practice. In considering what is appropriate to the speaker himself, Quintilian brings in a favorite topic of the philosophical schools, discussed for example in Cicero's *On Duties*, and earlier raised in connection with deliberative oratory, the possibility of conflict between what is expedient and what is honorable or fitting to the moral character of the speaker (XI,i,9). Naturally, to the perfect orator there is no real choice here. What is fitting will in the long run be expedient, and even if the conflict leads, as it did for Socrates, to death, the orator will gain immortal renown. Quintilian warns against boasting and defends Cicero against his critics with some rhetorical skill (XI,i,17–24).

To appropriateness to the speaker's character are added appropriateness in personifications, of which Cicero's introduction of old Appius Claudius into his speech for Caelius was the most famous, and appropriateness to a patron's client. A speech must suit both pleader and litigant (XI,i,42). This is analogous to the discussion of the varied function of patron and client which appeared in the chapter on the exordium.[49]

After looking at what is appropriate to speaker and client, Quintilian turns to the audience, the place, and the circumstances. To these he adds the opponent, quite logically, but this time fails to point out that both the opposing patron and his client are distinct factors as seen, for example, in Cicero's treatment of Hortensius and Verres in the trial of the latter.

The second half of the chapter is devoted to special problems (XI,i,48–93). How can particularly awkward subjects be handled, such as conflicts between parent and child or situations in which the judge has a personal hostility to the speaker? This, of course, is not really a matter of style, but of invention, as Quintilian realizes (XI,i, 78). The important problem of the hostility of an emperor is not specifically mentioned, but Quintilian's advice for dealing with hostile judges might represent his recommendation:

We shall feign that we have no fear because of our confidence in his justice and our right. He himself must be played upon through his love of adulation by stressing that his honor and prestige in giving judgment will be more celebrated the less he resents insult or indulges his self-interest. (XI,i,75)

The technique worked when applied by Cicero to Caesar, but its success with Caligula or Domitian is problematic. One of Quintilian's few direct references to the informers who figured so largely in contemporary oratory comes in this chapter when we are told that to attack another's fault which you admit to be also your own is the act of an informer, not of a pleader. Here, Quintilian uses *index*, the Ciceronian word for informer, rather then the common imperial term *delator* (XI,i,81). The chapter ends with stress on moderation and on the fact that cases will differ and virtues will differ with them.

At this point Quintilian has at last completed his discussion of style. Two parts of rhetoric remain, memory and delivery, and they are treated in the two remaining chapters of Book XI.

## V  *Memory*

The discussion of memory (XI,ii) is rather brief. There is first a short introduction: memory is a gift of nature improved by theory and practice, and without it all labor is wasted; the orator must remember not only his own speech, but the argument of his opponent. Then follows a famous story about Simonides of Ceos and his ability to remember people in a physical setting. Simonides was the reputed father of techniques of memory, and the story could have been continued into a historical review of the subject like the review of definitions of rhetoric or of stasis theory, but except for a reference to Metrodorus and Charmadas there is no further information. Cicero's *On the Orator* is Quintilian's primary source here, but he had read other discussions.

The system which Simonides invented and Metrodorus practiced was apparently the system of *imagines*, which we know best from a fairly clear description, with some examples, found at the end of the third book of the *Rhetoric to Herennius,* written about 84 B.C. The system involves the use of an extensive and familiar background, say a whole street, or, Quintilian suggests, the various rooms of a house. Visual memory of this background is permanently held in the mind, and against it images, representing different ideas or words, are imposed by the mind in a systematic order from one end to the other. When the orator comes to speak, he then imagines himself passing along the background and seeing the various images in turn. Each gives him a clue to what he has planned to say next. The same background can be used again and again, but the images vary with each work to be memorized. They may consist of actual people, like the litigants in a case, imagined doing something, or they may be symbolic, as a broken anchor might suggest a shipwreck. Quintilian was clearly familiar with this system and describes it briefly (XI,ii, 17–26), but he is unenthusiastic about it as a whole, and it would be almost impossible to learn to use it from his account.

Both in ancient and modern times a system of this sort has been employed by some people, but it seems cumbersome, especially if applied to a long speech. Quintilian felt that the images imposed a double task on the mind (XI,ii,25–26). Subsequently, he gives his own advice on how to memorize a speech, not a real system, but a series of practical suggestions (XI,ii,27–39). First of all, the speech should be divided up into parts, each to be learned separately. If individual passages prove difficult to remember, then the orator can try to use mnemonic devices, remembering a man's name by the literal meaning of his cognomen, for example, or can even adopt the system of *imagines* on a small scale and try to remember a set of symbols for the ideas or words of the passage. It will be helpful to memorize from the orator's own handwritten tablet, and thus to recall the appearance and position of the words on the page, though while practicing, the orator must be sure to speak words, not just to think them, so that eye, ear, and voice cooperate in the process of memorization (XI,ii,33). The logical divisions of the subject and its artistic structure will be invaluable in helping to hold it in mind. An attempt to memorize something should be spread out over at least one intervening night.

The biggest secret, however, is no real secret at all, but the need for constant practice. The more one memorizes, the more easily he will be able to memorize. It is generally preferable to memorize verbatim, Quintilian thinks, so that no word escapes, but sometimes it is adequate to memorize the essence and improvise words. The use of notes encourages carelessness in students and interruptions in the flow of the speech, and should not be permitted when a passage is supposedly memorized, though the use of notes by an adult orator had earlier been allowed (X,vii,31). In this chapter, Quintilian's concern is not with whether a speech should be delivered from memory or be extemporaneous, a subject discussed at the end of Book X, but with how to memorize a speech already composed, and he is primarily interested in how students can learn to memorize, not in the practice of adult orators. It is facility at memorization that helps make extemporization possible (XI,ii,3).

## VI  Delivery

Quintilian's account of delivery is the fullest discussion of that subject surviving from antiquity. At the beginning of the third book of the *Rhetoric*, Aristotle had pointed out that control of the voice had considerable significance, but had not been studied. He suggested that three qualities should be examined: volume, pitch, and rhythm. His pupil Theophrastus is supposed to have written a work on delivery, which may then have been elaborated by Hellenistic rhetoricians, as was Theophrastus' treatise on style, but we have very few direct references.[50] In the *Rhetoric to Herennius* there is a division of the subject into two topics which remained basic, voice and gesture, but voice was still given primary emphasis. A rather technical set of classifications of delivery is outlined: there are first conversation, debate, and amplification, and each of these, in turn, is broken down into subcategories.[51] Although Cicero knew these categories, his own discussions are less technical.[52]

Quintilian, as usual, follows the spirit of Cicero's remarks, but his account has certain special features. He makes the basic division into voice and gesture, but replaces volume, pitch, and rhythm with quantity and quality, both rather vaguely treated (XI,iii,14). He is, as one would expect, quite interested in the training of the voice and especially recommends learning varied passages by heart and practicing their delivery. The categories of the *Rhetoric to Herennius* are entirely ignored, and the discussion of voice is primarily structured on four qualities which are identical with the four virtues of style of Books VIII and IX (XI,iii,30). That delivery should be parallel to style is logical, but Quintilian has some difficulty in adapting the four virtues. Clarity and propriety present no problems, but in demanding correctness Quintilian seems unclear whether he is demanding merely absence of fault or some positive virtue, and if so how that differs from those which follow (XI,iii,30–32). Ornamentation is defined as smoothness and variety, and the latter is analogous to a figure, for it is compared to varied positions taken by the body (XI,iii,44). Since Quintilian does not claim originality for his adaptation of the virtues of style to delivery, it is likely that he had found it elsewhere, but he doesn't say where. Among the most interesting parts of the discussion are examinations of the correct delivery of the opening of the *Aeneid* and of Cicero's speech for Milo, showing in both cases how the sentences should be punctuated and in the latter case what tones should be used (XI,iii,36–38; 47–51).

Quintilian's account of gesture (XI,iii,65–144) is our best literary source on what an ancient orator looked like while giving a speech.[53] A moderate as always, he makes it clear that some orators went far beyond anything which he approves. His discussion starts with the movement of the head, moves down past neck, shoulders, and arms to the hands, then reaches the feet and the motion of the whole body, and concludes with remarks on how to manage the toga, no small challenge in itself. Certain general principles seem to emerge. The eyes (XI,iii,72) and the hands (XI,iii,85) are regarded as the most important parts. Motion should ordinarily be from the left to the right (XI,iii,106), the eye following through the same motion as does the hand (XI,iii,70). The left hand may be used in conjunction with the right, but not alone (XI,iii,114). Ordinarily, gestures should not go above the level of the eye, or below the breast (XI,iii,112), or left of the shoulder (XI,iii,113), though in moments of great emotion the thigh may be struck with the right hand (XI,iii,123). Gesture should be suited to the words, but should not mimic actions conveyed by words (XI,iii,88–91). The process should be disciplined, yet spontaneous: gesture should not be planned at the time of composition (XI,iii,109). Whether or not walking about is suitable depends largely on the arrangement and size of the court: an orator may need to walk along the front of the bench addressing a large jury (XI,iii,130). It is perfectly proper for the toga to become disarranged in the course of a speech (XI,iii,144 and 148).

After examining the different kinds of gesture, Quintilian returns to the subject of what is appropriate in delivery and considers the various parts of a speech and the different kinds of speakers. Here he describes in some detail how an orator should conduct himself (XI,iii,156–174). When called, he rises and secures a few moments for reflection while he arranges his toga. He then turns to the judge, but still does not launch into his speech. A dramatic tension is built up as he strokes his head, or looks at his hands, or even sighs. Then, his feet slightly apart, standing straight but not stiffly, his face serious but not sad, his arms slightly out from the body, his right hand extending from the folds of his toga before his breast, its thumb upward, fingers slightly bent, ready to move out toward the right, he begins to speak, calmly, with dignity, seeking the sympathy and good will of the jury. In his narration, the gestures become more marked, the voice sharper; the proof requires great variety, but is apt to take still more energy, interspersed perhaps with a serene and picturesque digression. There are many different kinds of perorations, and the orator's task is to find the delivery natural for the particular case. Some examples are considered. The passage as a whole is a fascinating statement of the purely esthetic side of listening to an ancient orator, and it makes a fine artistic conclusion to Quintilian's long account of rhetoric. The orator is ready for actual combat.

# CHAPTER 5

## *Quintilian as a Critic*

THE most famous and most read portion of Quintilian's work is the tenth book. Its function within the *Institutio* as a whole is to explain how an orator is to take a step beyond his knowledge of rules and theory in order to attain facility at speaking. The objective is thus practical and educational. Though a good deal of literary criticism is involved in what Quintilian says, and much of the interest of the book arises from that fact, he writes from the same point of view as ever and has not suddenly converted himself into a literary critic. Indeed, no such profession existed at Rome.

Facility can be attained through reading, writing, and speaking. Thus each of these is examined, as are also the contributions of imitation, emendation, and premeditation to the creative faculty. The book is unusual in a rhetorical treatise, and, like Quintilian's account of elementary education or of the adult orator, should be viewed as an expansion of the subject through inclusion of material more often treated in separate monographs. Though implicitly foreshadowed in the promise of the preface of Book I to nourish eloquence, it is unexpectedly inserted into the middle of the discussion of style, separating the account of the third virtue, ornamentation, from the fourth virtue, appropriateness. This is certainly not the only place where it could have been put, but it is the earliest place. By facility, Quintilian has in mind first of all facility at finding the right word, and though reading will also provide examples of thought and invention, its first and most vital task is to produce word power. Concern for word power is certainly very closely connected with ornamentation and can logically follow after that topic, and perhaps it logically precedes discussion of how to use appropriately the power which has been acquired. But Quintilian found it convenient to group writing and speaking together with reading, and this leads him to some topics which would have been better postponed until he has finished not only with appropriateness, but with memory and delivery. As he himself says (X,i,4), in Book X he is no longer thinking about the formal education of the orator, but of how one who has learned all the rules and become a trained athlete of speech can be prepared for actual contests. Yet in Book XI he is again discussing the rules. The order of Books X and XI thus could have been reversed with some logic. Indeed, there is also a logical tie between the reading demanded in Book X and the knowledge of philosophy and history examined in Book XII. It is tempting to deduce here signs of haste or carelessness in composition, but it is clear that Quintilian desired to emphasize the contents of Book X, and possibly he practices a kind of hyperbaton in putting it in the earliest possible place in his work.

For facility in speaking the orator must have a ready supply of subjects and words, and these he will attain by reading (X,i,5). Quintilian rather dismisses subjects at first as of less general utility than are words, but later it is made clear that the student will find in his reading application of all the rhetorical precepts which he has studied (X,i,15). Thus, though he will enlarge his vocabulary and learn how to use words and commonplaces appropriately, he will also discover something about how to argue, how to deploy emotional elements, how to arrange material, what effects are possible through figures or composition, and the like. It is of course method, not substance, which will most engage his attention. Though he may appreciate the greatness of what he reads, his object is imitation and the practical utilization in his own work of what he sees in the work of others. The first part of the chapter also couples reading and listening, but Quintilian thinks careful judgment of what is spoken is not really possible, since speech is too vivid, too rapid, too much affected by voice and gesture, and the listener is too much influenced by the character of the speaker (X,i,17). Critical analysis is only possible after careful reading and rereading of a text. The point is well taken and may even be one of the reasons why the critical faculty was not highly developed in antiquity. Poetry and prose were ordinarily read aloud, even in private, and appreciation took precedence over analysis.

Since his point of view is that of a teacher of public speaking, not of a critic, Quintilian never finds it necessary to outline in detail a system of rhetorical criticism. How he would go about analyzing a work is, however, fairly clear from his description of how to teach literature (II,v,5–9) and from what he says throughout the *Institutio*.

He would, in a word, follow the traditional rhetorical categories. Understanding stasis and its effect on strategy and arrangement would be an important part of the study. The various stylistic devices should be analyzed and their contribution to the intention of the speaker appreciated. Here in Book X some general advice is given for approaching all works of literature (X,i,20–26). They should, for example, be read all the way through, and their unity should be appreciated, especially the way a good writer mentions something early in a work and then takes it up again later on. Before approaching a work, the student must be sure that he has adequate background knowledge to understand it. In the case of oratory, it is especially valuable to read, if possible, opposing speeches in the same case. After these prefatory remarks, Quintilian turns to the question of what to read, and thus to a review of Greek and Latin literature, genre by genre and author by author.

This famous discussion raises a number of problems. How well did Quintilian himself know the literature he discusses? What sources does he follow, either in the classification and canonization of authors or in individual judgments? What are his general views of literature, and must what he says be viewed only in connection with his particular purpose in this book, or does it represent a more general evaluation? Is he conscious of having left out certain authors and of having treated others superficially? Exactly what does he mean by the epithets applied to particular authors or works? What is his view of the relation of Greek to Latin? The answers to these questions may be partly derived from what we have observed already about Quintilian's methods, objectives, and tastes, and from literary conditions at the time he wrote.

If we follow the order of his own discussion, the first problems to arise involve the nature and function of poetry, history, and philosophy, all of which the orator is urged to read. Since Quintilian constantly refers to poets, especially Virgil, and historians, most frequently Sallust, and occasionally to philosophers like Socrates, Plato, or the Stoics, he seems to have followed his own advice. The study of the poets was a regular part of grammar school education, and Quintilian had earlier urged that history and oratory be read in the earlier stages of the rhetorical school (II,v). Now he wants the advanced student to continue or to resume his reading. Many other rhetoricians shared his view, he says (X,i,27).

What the orator is to learn from the poet, according to Quintilian (X,i,27–30), is inspired treatment of the subject, sublimity of expression, emotional power, and character presentation, and he will also find poetry a pleasant form of relaxation. Quintilian goes on, however, to warn that a poet has much greater freedom in the choice of words and use of figures than does an orator, for the poet has the demands of his verse form to consider and he writes for show. Gold and silver are suited to the poet, the steel of battle to the orator. Indeed, Quintilian goes so far as to say that poetry *solam petit voluptatem*, "aims at pleasure alone." How broadly does he mean this judgment, which, if pressed, would seem to condemn poetry to entertainment and triviality?

In the context, it is clear that he is speaking chiefly about style. Whatever the poet's material, he always should seek euphony, harmony, and rhythm, never harshness, whereas the orator will seek softness or roughness as the situation requires. This is basically what is meant by pursuing pleasure. As far as subject matter goes, Quintilian regarded all literature, including poetry, as capable of some serious purpose. He has just spoken of the inspired treatment of the subject, vague as that phrase is, as part of poetry, and in the discussion of individual Greek and Latin poets there is often reference to something other than style: the moral force with which Alcaeus attacked tyrants is praised, for example (X,i,63), and we are told that Macer and Lucretius should be read, but not for their style (X,i,87); there must therefore be something else. On the other hand, there is no expression of the old concept, voiced at Rome chiefly by Horace,[1] of the poet as teacher, preacher, and prophet, no express recognition that a poet like Virgil may have a cause to plead or a view of life to express which gives him a public function analogous to that of an orator. The orator as a practical man cannot forsake real life; the poet on the other hand is set in direct opposition to him: he can isolate himself from the world in the pursuit of pleasure.

When Quintilian discusses particular poets, he reveals a sympathy for what might be called the constructive poets of the empire. The sort of poet he perhaps most approved is represented by Valerius Flaccus, whose recent death he laments (X,i,90). In Valerius' work there can be found attempts at character portrayal, at emotion, at sublimity of expression, all within traditional lines. What Quintilian presumably meant by inspired treatment is there too, in the epic scope and heroic subject, which is the expedition of Jason and the Argonauts, complete with all the resources of religion and mythology. At the same time there is occasional reference in a complimentary way to Rome of the Flavians, and doubtless there would have been more if Valerius had lived to finish the work. This is what poetry should be, pleasurable, even exciting, but loyal and with no awkward tensions. In contrast, Quintilian found the work of the pleasure-loving Ovid undisciplined (X,i,88), while Lucan's epic, quite the opposite, seemed to him more oratorical than poetic (X,i, 90): its political and historical subject was still pointedly relevant, for Lucan was pleading a real cause, and the style was cacophonous and violent. His work had force, but not charm. Valerius thus represents a satisfactory mean. There is something timid in a critical approach that can reject Ovid and Lucan in favor of Valerius Flaccus, but to do Quintilian justice we must remember that all these writers were in his opinion far inferior to Virgil, and to judge from his quotations, it is not Virgil's imperial propaganda, but the magic of his lines which he loved.

Quintilian also seems to take a restricted view of the function of history, which he says is of all prose forms the closest to poetry, aiming at narration, not at proof, and composed to preserve memory of the past and secure fame for the writer (X,i,31–34). Though Sallust and Livy are cited, the political interests of the one and the moral purpose of the other are both ignored. Others may admire Cremutius Cordus, but Quintilian has no words of regret for the passages of his works excised by the imperial censors.[2] An orator, he says, will chiefly imitate historians in digressions and will, of course, find a knowledge of history useful in his proofs. Strangely, nothing is said here about the oratory which constitutes such an important part of ancient historiography, though the speeches in Thucydides and Livy are later praised (X,i,73–101). Quintilian must have read Cicero's remarks on historical literature, but has either failed to understand them or has deliberately reduced the significant and thus the controversial element in history.[3] Here he stands in opposition to Tacitus, who a few years after publication of the *Institutio* was to abandon the goal of the orator as no longer practicable and to seek an opportunity for significant expression in historical writing. It is impossible to think that Quintilian would have approved either the disjointed style or the bitter spirit of Tacitus.

Thirdly, the orator will read philosophy (X,i,35–36). Quintilian's views here are not so much restricted as hostile, and are thus consistent with his attitude toward philosophy elsewhere in his work. There would, he thinks, have been no need to turn to the philosophers if the orators had lived up to their duty.

Quintilian's views of the various literary genres are thus not very well thought out and represent various prejudices of his time. In his consideration of what to read, he next turns to specific authors, which means Cicero and Demosthenes more than anyone else, but something can be gained from almost every author. He takes up Greek literature genre by genre; within each genre he usually cites the most important author first, then comments on others in roughly chronological order. Early in the discussion (X,i,54) he refers to a canon of writers of epic and iambic verse drawn up by the grammarians, naming Aristarchus and Aristophanes of Byzantium specifically, and thus it seems likely that his choice of writers and the order of the discussion[4] are influenced by critical lists dating from the Hellenistic period and originally emanating from the libraries of Alexandria or Pergamum. The point of such lists was to indicate, sometimes in order of quality, the writers of a particular genre whom a librarian or grammarian approved and recommended and whose works belonged in a library. The most famous extant list is the so-called canon of the ten Attic orators, the exact origin of which is not known. Quintilian may have it in mind in one passage (X,i,76), but names only five of the ten and, under Cicero's influence, adds Demetrius of Phaleron who was not on the list.[5] As elsewhere in Quintilian's work, Cicero's influence is pervasive, but not overwhelming. Quintilian shows familiarity with, but does not slavishly follow, the accounts of orators in the *Brutus* and of historians and orators in *On the Orator*.[6] The biggest difference between Cicero and Quintilian here is not the different writers who are mentioned, or the scale of the treatment, but the fact that Cicero regularly stresses historical development from author to author, where Quintilian takes a much more static view of each genre.[7] This is due partly to the fact that he is drawing up a reading list, not writing literary history. Cicero was much interested in the development of Latin literature, which was still going on in his own time, whereas Quintilian thought that not only Greek, but Latin had achieved a certain plateau. What has been done in the past can be rivaled, perfected, perhaps even surpassed, but fundamental change or a development of new forms is not really anticipated. One sign of this is that all literature is regarded as embraced within the traditional genres.

The only surviving precedent for Quintilian's discussion of Greek authors is the work of Dionysius of Halicarnassus, *On Imitation*. Quintilian does not refer to this, though he may have read it at some time since Dionysius was well known to him (III,i,16). The parallels between what Dionysius says and Quintilian's chapter are great enough to suggest that we are dealing with a recognized traditional topic, but not close enough to prove that Quintilian has copied Dionysius.[8] Another discussion of what to read is the eighteenth oration of Dio Chrysostom. Dio's list is intended as a kind of cram course for a public official whose education has been neglected. It proceeds by genres, but in a different order from Quintilian's account, and agrees with some of Quintilian's estimates, for example on Menander, Homer, and Demosthenes, but puts remarkable emphasis on Xenophon. Quintilian doubtless knew of Dio, but he certainly did not copy him and it is quite possible that Dio's speech dates from a time after the publication of the *Institutio*.

Quintilian had learned Greek as a young man, and his knowledge of the language was certainly good enough to enable him to understand and talk to Greek rhetoricians. He clearly had read the more recent Greek theorists like Caecilius (IX,i,12), but some Greek critics were apparently available in Latin translations or summaries (II,xv,21; III,i,18). His knowledge of earlier Greek rhetoricians, however, could have been gained through secondary sources: no one read the crabbed Hermagoras in the original if he could help it, and what Quintilian got from Theophrastus could have come through Cicero or other sources. But it seems perverse to assume that he did not himself know Aristotle's *Rhetoric*, and at least one reference (V,x,17) indicates that he may have read it through at some time.[9] Further, he criticizes those who read Plato's *Gorgias* only in excerpts, and perhaps he was accustomed to lecture on that work in his school (II,xv,24–28). In the age in which he lived, Greek books were commonly available in libraries at Rome, public and private, and still widely read,[10] and though Quintilian hardly rivaled Plutarch or the elder Pliny as a reader, his commitment was to the literary life; he takes a historical approach to rhetorical problems and could not have maintained his reputation as he did without extensive reading.

Was this reading in Greek restricted to rhetoricians? A passage in Book VIII (vi,71) suggests that he was particularly fond of Pindar; he even preserves a fragment of Pindar otherwise unknown (X,i, 109). Many of his quotations or examples from Greek literature (and they are not especially numerous to start with) he could, however, have derived from other rhetoricians, either Greek or Latin. Examples of technique tended to become traditional, and Quintilian's literary judgments are certainly traditional (e.g., X,i,53–54). It was to be expected from his character, and he was well aware of it. He certainly did not undertake a careful and independent critical estimate of Greek literature. Except for Pindar, his tastes are those of a rhetorician: Homer and Menander, Euripides rather than Sophocles, the orators, especially Demosthenes, whose works, he says, should be learned by heart (X,i,105). He does not forget why he is writing and is aware that other writers of merit exist (X,i,45): thus the omission of a name, that of Sappho for example, only means that he does not think an author particularly useful to an orator. On the other hand, his low estimate of Aratus is surprising (X,i,55), for that poet was admired and translated by Cicero and other Romans.

In reviewing appropriate Latin literature, Quintilian follows the form and order of his Greek survey. He had the example of Cicero's discussion of Roman orators and historians as compared to the Greek and at least one list of Roman comic poets by order of merit, the so-called canon of Volcacius Sedigitus,[11] but many of the writers he has to discuss are later than Cicero or Volcacius and he obviously knew them well at first hand. His Latin judgments thus seem more independent than his Greek. As before, most of the judgments are not absolute ones, but estimates of the utility of a writer for training an orator, though this fact emerges in a rather strangely backhanded way in the case of Lucan, whom Quintilian did not like as a poet, but had to admit was rhetorical. His admiration for Virgil and Cicero is to be expected, and his praise of Sallust is consistent with what he says elsewhere. Catullus' name appears only among the iambic poets (X,i,96), not among the lyric or elegiac, and probably he would have relatively little to contribute to an orator, though Quintilian quotes him occasionally elsewhere. It is interesting to see how little Quintilian thought of Roman comedy (X,i,99); the point here is not the lack of originality of Roman comic poets, but the deficiencies of the Latin language as compared to the charm of the Greek of Menander and others. Indeed, one sign of Virgil's genius is that he was equal to the task of writing in Latin.[12] Quintilian explains in Book XII that the problem is partly one of the harsher sound of Latin, partly its limited vocabulary (XII,x,27–39). He does not ever discuss the problems of originality in Latin literature, though, as we will see, he does consider the difficulties of vying in quality with what has gone before.

Many of Quintilian's succinct and memorable statements about Latin writers have become part of traditional criticism and are still enshrined in present-day histories of Latin literature. Ennius' fragments still seem to us what they seemed to Quintilian, an ancient grove of oaks, not so much beautiful as inspiring religious awe (X,i,

88). "There are those who prefer Propertius" effectively damned
that worthy author until "those" came to include Ezra Pound. "Satire
is wholly ours" *(ibid.)* has become the classic statement of its Roman
origin; Terentius Varro is still called "the most learned of the Romans" (X,i,95); there is still noted the "immortal rapidity of Sallust"
(X,i,102), "the milky richness" of Livy having been mentioned earlier
in the chapter (X,i,32). The critical epithets are intended to be self-
evident and non-technical; indeed, the idea of a well-defined critical
vocabulary is entirely foreign to Quintilian. We can agree that
Tibullus is "terse and elegant" (X,i,93) without attributing exact
meanings to those words. Sometimes Quintilian's terms are capable
of being misunderstood. For example, "Macer and Lucretius certainly ought to be read, but not to form *phrasis,* that is, the body of
style; each is elegant in his own material, but the former is *humilis*
and the latter *difficilis*" (X,i,87). "Elegant" suggests careful choice
of what is to be included, what rejected, but the result is hardly the
same as in Tibullus, where the elegance is more in the diction. In
the last part of the sentence Quintilian seems to have transferred to
the author what he means to say of the subject: Macer wrote on
pedestrian subjects *(humilis),* didactic poems on birds, animal bites,
and plants, and similarly it is not that Quintilian found Lucretius
difficult to understand, but that Lucretius' subject, atoms and void,
was an intractable one *(difficilis).*

Three passages call for special comment. The first is the discussion
of Roman epic (X,i,85–92), already mentioned. It begins with Virgil,
whom Quintilian clearly appreciated, and whom he had discussed
with Domitius Afer, but in fact says nothing about the qualities or
passages in Virgil which will be most significant for an orator.
Probably Quintilian thought the matter was self-evident from the
many citations of Virgil throughout the *Institutio.* Then follows a
discussion of other, chiefly later, epic poets. They are inferior to
Virgil, of course, but no general poetic decline is remarked, nor is
there any specific indication of the controversy which had raged
over epic when Quintilian was a young man and Lucan had startled
the world by publishing an epic not only remarkable in diction and
composition, but omitting the traditional interventions of the gods.
Nor is there any discussion of the differences between mythological,
historical, and didactic epic. But some hints can be found between
the lines. Ovid's manner in epic is not highly approved; presumably
Quintilian is thinking of the *Metamorphoses.* On the other hand,
there is more praise for a series of now lost poets who wrote chiefly

on recent historical themes from a loyal and constructive point of view, and there is praise for the mythological work of Valerius Flaccus. Lucan is a problem: as a poet he is not approved, but as a rhetorician he is. Whether Quintilian is thinking chiefly of style or subject is not said. He might well have disliked some aspects of both, including Lucan's unsympathetic treatment of Cicero, his fiery republicanism, and the fact that his verse is a counterpart to Seneca's prose.

There then follows a passage in which Quintilian breaks his custom of never naming a living author to sing the praise of the poetry of the reigning emperor, Domitian, or rather the praise of the promise shown in what Domitian had written before more important things intervened. As a bit of flattery, the passage is rivaled only by the invocation of the emperor and praise of his eloquence in the preface to Book IV, though it is not remarkable when compared to the adulation in other writers. At the beginning of his father's reign Domitian initially had had the advantage of being in Rome whereas both Vespasian and Titus had been far away in the East, but then he had been pushed aside. He felt hurt, but pretended that he voluntarily withdrew into a life of writing, leaving administration of the state to his father and brother.[13] Not only Quintilian, but Valerius Flaccus, Silius Italicus, and Statius go out of their way to show that they believe this and to praise Domitian's poetry.[14] The presence of the reference in the restrained Quintilian would seem to mean that Domitian was very touchy on the subject, and that there was some danger that an informer might accuse Quintilian of slighting the emperor. It is possible that Quintilian felt epic poetry to be a particularly ticklish subject because of its political implications and thought that it could be most safely discussed if accompanied by a certain amount of flag waving. The praise of Domitian certainly overshadows the remarks about Lucan which immediately preceded, if they can be imagined to be in any way dangerous.

A second portion of special interest is naturally that on oratory, the literary form in which Quintilian believes the Romans had most successfully rivaled the Greeks (X,i,105–122). Some of his remarks are further amplified later (XII,i,14–22 and x). Comparison of Demosthenes and Cicero was a standard feature of critical writing in the Roman Empire, possibly the best known today being that in the work *On Sublimity*, attributed to Longinus. Quintilian clearly prefers Cicero, despite the inferiority of the Latin language, on the ground that he has most of the virtues of Demosthenes, but more wit and pathos. The difference in style between the two is well summed up in the *sententia* that from Demosthenes' expression nothing can be taken away, to Cicero's nothing can be added. Cicero is presented as the more varied writer, capable of attaining something like the virtues of a Plato or an Isocrates as well as those of Demosthenes. Quintilian's love of Cicero is at root a personal matter, a sympathetic understanding of many of Cicero's basic feelings about what an orator ought to be, about his constructive duties in society, about the great power and art inherent in words. He does not share Cicero's personal drive or creativity, though he admires them. Cicero's philosophical inclination he lacks. This native sympathy with Cicero may have been encouraged by Domitius Afer and sharpened by the antipathy which Quintilian felt for the "new style," the manner of most declaimers and of Seneca and his imitators, who shunned Cicero's fullness and rhythm and sought speed and *sententiae*. Furthermore, fashions in prose style tend to follow patterns of reaction. Just as reaction against Cicero's style was likely in the early empire,[15] so reaction against the declamatory style could be predicted as it grew tiresome and as Cicero took on the aura of a noble Roman of the great past. Most of the writers of the Flavian age are more "classic" than those of the Neronian period. Among prose writers, Quintilian appears to be the leader in neo-Ciceronianism, given an advantage because of his official position. It is thus natural to attribute the relatively Ciceronian features of the style of the younger Pliny to his studies with Quintilian. The most Ciceronian work of the age is probably the *Dialogue on the Orators* by Tacitus, a work which challenges Quintilian's fundamental position, and in which the Ciceronian style is almost ironically suitable. To spell out the stylistic objectives of the devious mind of Tacitus is impossible here, but the choice of style certainly shows interest in Ciceronian prose. In his historical works, Tacitus wrote in quite a different manner.

It must be stressed that Quintilian's admiration for Cicero leads him to take Cicero as a touchstone of taste, an inspiration, a general example of what can be done, a source of illustration or precept, but not as a dictator of good style. Quintilian's writing is Ciceronian as compared to Seneca's, but constantly employs words and constructions and rhetorical mannerisms which are part of the language of the first century A.D., but not to be found in Cicero, just as his rhetorical theory contains points not found in Cicero. Quintilian believes that times change and with them both taste and linguistic usages: by imperial standards Cicero is lacking in *sententiae*.[16] Quintilian does not want to go back or to try to maintain a specific standard by arbitrary rules. He wants a natural evolution to prevail. The extreme declamatory style is to him unnatural; writing in the Ciceronian tradition is far more natural. To regard Quintilian as a reactionary is thus not really fair; he is a traditionalist who wants to keep tradition vigorous. A sign of this is that unlike others he does not believe that there has been any general literary decline in the empire. There has not been a writer so good as Cicero, but there may yet be. For all his virtues Cicero is not the absolute perfection which might conceivably be attained, especially with the shifts of time. Many orators of the empire are thus included in the account of Latin oratory as worthy models: "There are today," he says, "great geniuses who add luster to the forum. And splendid patrons [orators] now rival the ancients and inspire the imitation and industry of the ambitious young" (X,i,122).[17] Furthermore, no sharp line is drawn between ancients and moderns. In this respect, Quintilian belongs with Aper, the modernist in Tacitus' *Dialogue,* who tries to show that Cicero should be grouped with the modern orators.[18]

A third passage which deserves special note furnishes a natural contrast to the praise of Cicero; this is the discussion of Seneca, by whom is meant the younger Seneca, the philosopher and dramatist, adviser to Nero (X,i,125–31). Quintilian protests against the idea, common in Rome, that he has been totally antipathetic to Seneca, and insists in turn on Seneca's intelligence, zeal, and knowledge. Though he does not remark it, there is a tie between them in that each had sought to work for what he believed in by cooperation with and support of the emperor, and Seneca demonstrates an example of what Quintilian seems to regard as the opportunities for an orator under the empire. Furthermore, Quintilian's moral and philosophical views tended toward Seneca's, though they are less developed and less extreme. The problem with Seneca, in Quintilian's view, is his prose style, and especially his pursuit of novelty and brevity. Moreover, like Ovid, he had gloried in his vices and disparaged the style of others. Quintilian cannot stand lack of control or backbiting. Indeed, his whole discussion is a typical attempt to be fair. The biggest problem is represented as not Seneca himself, but ignorant and tasteless attempts to ape him by boys in rhetorical schools. He should be read, but by adults, not by impressionable young men. This is probably fair enough, considering the pressures within the rhetorical schools to be clever and showy, though there is more to be said for Seneca's style than Quintilian can admit, and to Seneca himself it was the one thing Quintilian denies it to be, a natural form of expression, natural to his character and view of the world, and that is not a bad thing for style to be.[19]

## I  *Imitation*

As we have said, the object of the orator's reading is practical. He is to acquire a knowledge of words, devices of style, and treatment of subject matter for his own use. He will thus imitate the writers whom he studies. What is now the second chapter of Book X discusses this important and historic subject more directly. It is one of the best and most significant parts of Quintilian's work.

The word "imitation" is used in different senses by ancient critics. First of all, there is imitation of nature as the basis of most art, in the sense that a play imitates life. Menander was regarded as particularly successful at this. A related concept is Plato's notion of the visible world as being an imitation of the real world of the forms. Quintilian was aware of these meanings, but primarily uses the word, as does Dionysius of Halicarnassus in his essay on the subject, in the sense of imitation of literary models.[20] Imitation is thus a principle of literary creativity. Other principles had been defined at different times. In early Greek thinking, for example, inspiration seems to figure strongly, though we can now see that in fact early Greek poets, especially oral poets, composed with heavy reliance on imitation. Then, in classical Greece, theories of criticism and specific rules of poetry or rhetoric were formulated and observance of them was regarded as creating an acceptable literary product. Any one of these principles might be, probably should be, accompanied by emendation and polishing, what Horace called the *limae labor,* or "work of the file." [21] Quintilian is aware of these various principles. Inspiration he thinks of sometimes as "nature," the single most important quality, but something not much can be done about (X,vii, 14), or else as a matter of emotion and imagination. Rules, of course, make up most of the *Institutio*. Emendation will be discussed in what is now chapter iv.

Imitation, according to Quintilian, is entirely natural: it is the way one learns to read and write in the first place. All learning is directed to some prescribed standard, he says (X,ii,2). We must either be like or unlike what is good. This suggests that the doctrine of imitation implies a rather static conception of the good in various literary genres, something vaguely like imitation as Plato conceived it, but since Quintilian speaks of the good in the plural and appears to mean individual good models, not an abstract principle, we cannot fairly accuse him of trying to direct all imitation toward a single model as the perfect form in each genre (see X,v,5–6). Indeed, his actual position allows for a good deal of variety since he recognizes changes in taste and usage and insists strongly on the need to adapt a particular work to its particular circumstances.

The doctrine of imitation may also be thought to imply classicism. Even if there is no abstract good model, there are the great works of the past which we can imitate, though hardly equal. Quintilian is drawn to this view by his admiration for Homer, Demosthenes, and Menander among the Greeks and for Cicero and Virgil among the Romans, but he fights against it. There is to his mind no logical reason why such should be the case; as has been said, unlike some writers of the first century, he will not admit the reality of literary decline resulting from fate, literary cycles, or political conditions. Bad writing there has been, under the influence of bad models and bad teachers, but good writing too, and the greatest may yet be. He is thus led to write a very significant passage cautioning against the dangers and limitations of imitation (X,ii,4–13). Imitation of literary classics is not enough; literature would never have arisen in the first place if there had been nothing but imitation, and why should we not be as inventive and original as primitive man? As it is, we have the advantage of the past and should build on it. It is the nature of the arts to develop. We must not condemn our own age as incapable of progress! All models, good as they are, still have some blemish, some room for improvement. A man can never surpass or even equal another if he only tries to follow him. And it is actually easier to surpass than exactly to equal what has been done. Imitation will necessarily lack the natural force and vigor of an original creation, some qualities cannot be imitated at all, and many imitators are too easily content with reproducing trivialities. Words go out of use, and art must suit its occasion, not copy some obsolete standard.

Creativity then must go beyond imitation. It must have a life and force of its own, disciplined and inspired by what has been done, but suited to its own time and place. Fundamental change in literary tradition is not envisioned, but continual perfecting is possible. In imitating, we must be sure that we distinguish real excellences from mannerisms. An orator who ends all his periods with *esse videatur* deceives himself if he thinks he is imitating the rhythmical virtues of Cicero (X,ii,18). Next, we must not pursue virtues totally foreign to our own nature. If our abilities are in the simple style, we may try to enlarge our scope somewhat, but we should not incongruously strive for the direct opposite of what we do well. If we are imitating a model outside the genre in which we are working, it is necessary to be especially careful that the qualities we select are not something peculiar to that genre, but are a common element of all eloquence. We must be varied and adaptable to need, and thus imitation of a single style is usually inadequate: we need several models.

This raises the particular problem of the imitation of Cicero (X,ii, 25–26). Throughout the work, he is represented as the greatest and most varied of writers. Is he not adequate as an object of imitation for an orator? The answer would appear to be that he is nearly so, but not quite. He has all the virtues, but not at all times, and of course he wrote for his own age. For effective oratory in Quintilian's time, more *sententiae* would be advisable (XII,x,46). Certain oratorical characteristics are more generally manifest in some other writers. Suppose a student of oratory feels particularly in need of force *(vis)*. Now there is much force in Cicero, but it is more constantly and pervasively a characteristic of Caesar, and the student may thus be better off studying Caesar in this respect. A particular quality in Cicero may be so blended with others that its true source will be impossible to analyze. In practice, then, the orator will use imitation to counteract his own weakness while building on his native strengths to produce the best possible work for the age in which he lives. He engages in a kind of emulation with the virtues of the past.

In the conclusion of the chapter, Quintilian spells out slightly more what it is that is to be imitated. He has already mentioned use of words, figures, and rhythms, and overall qualities like force or severity or earnestness, not always suitable of course; now he adds appropriate treatment of subjects and persons, judgment, arrangement, the way in which everything, even a seeming digression, contributes to the objective, specific techniques in the various divisions of the speech, and utilization of the audience's reaction (X,ii,27). In other words, the student must engage in an analytic study of his models, then consciously try to do the same or a similar thing. The technique of imitation is one reason for the large number of literary allusions and similarities to be found and intended to be consciously savored not only in Latin, but in much of Renaissance and some of modern literature, like Joyce or Pound. Western literature, as Quintilian already recognized, is a continuous tradition.

The rest of Book X is concerned with practice in writing and speaking, first taking up writing, then emendation, forms of exercise in composition, premeditation, and extempore speaking. Quintilian wants a student to write with care and believes that he can gradually learn to write with speed (X,iii,10). A few matters touched upon were apparently somewhat controversial. For writing material, Quintilian recommends waxed tablets since they can easily be erased, but if the eye is weak, ink and parchment will be better (X,iii,31). Space must be left for corrections, and the writer must also have a place to keep notes relating to portions of the work not yet written. Dio Chrysostom recommends dictation,[22] but Quintilian is strongly against it as making for hasty composition or conversely, if the secretary is slow, as checking the flow, and in any event as inhibiting the writer's expression of emotion (X,iii,19–21). It is best to be alone when writing. This does not mean that one should be in some kind of idyllic setting, which might well be distracting (X,iii,22). What is best is simply privacy and quiet, which may mean that writing has to be done at night. But a writer ought not to pamper himself; he will have to speak in the busy forum and he should learn to concentrate wherever he is: in a crowd, on a trip, at social gatherings, his thoughts should have some secret corner of his mind (X,iii, 30). Quintilian always assumes that will power can accomplish anything. Emendation is important and most effective if some time has elapsed, but it can be overdone and a reasonably good draft left in tatters (X,iv,3). A writer should try to write well enough the first time so that only polishing is necessary. This is consistent with what Quintilian had said of the writing of his own work in the prefatory letter to his bookseller.

The discussion of exercises in composition (X,v) builds on what has been said in Books I and II and also on the contributions of poetry and history as discussed earlier in Book X. Translations from Greek into Latin, paraphrases of poetry or even oratory, and development of theses are all recommended. One reason for Cicero's greatness in style is said to have been his practice in writing dialogues and verse as well as oratory (X,v,16). To counteract the artificiality of declamation, the student should choose varied and realistic subjects, but should also attend the law courts and should compose practice speeches on the cases which he hears. He should select some practicing orator to follow and imitate, which Quintilian had done himself in the person of Domitius Afer.

By premeditation (X,vi) is meant the planning of a speech ahead of time; it must then be held in the memory for delivery. The opposite is extempore speaking (X,vii). At times this will be absolutely essential for the practicing orator if he is to defend the client's interest, and it is a logical objective of his training and exercise to be able to speak at any moment. What will help first will be a clear understanding of the logic of the case, an avoidance of the irrelevant, and a careful division of the subject, faithfully carried out, but actual effective expression requires that facility at which both reading and writing, as discussed elsewhere, have aimed. Constant practice is essential, and the mental images discussed in Book VI will be helpful in producing a vivid fluency (X,vii,15).

The topic of extempore speech naturally leads over into the question of preparation and thus of memorization, and Quintilian concludes his discussion with some interesting historical comments on the customs of orators. Cicero, he says (X,vii,30), commonly wrote out the beginnings of his speeches, planned the rest in his mind, and trusted to improvisation, if necessary. Most orators, however, seem to have written out whole speeches and memorized them, and this was the procedure ordinarily taught in the rhetorical schools. Sometimes speaker's notes, *commentarii* they were called, were subsequently published, sometimes a speaker wrote up a revised version of his speech for posterity. Notes on particular matters, relevant financial details in a private case might be an example, can be held in the hand, Quintilian says. On the other hand, he disapproves of an orator imperfectly memorizing a speech and trying to speak from an outline, since he will flounder about unevenly between his original version and what he can otherwise think of to say (X,vii,31–33).

All of this discussion logically belongs in Book XI with the rules of memorization and delivery. It shows how varied is the material of Book X, and how Quintilian's attention continually comes back to the one thing that really interests him, the teaching of effective public speaking. He is more a practicing teacher than an educational theorist, more an educational theorist than a critic.

As a matter of fact, the chapter in which Quintilian comes closest to writing pure criticism is not in Book X at all, but is the tenth chapter of Book XII. That book is devoted to the complete and perfected orator, and this particular chapter to the styles in which he will speak and thus to the work of art which he will produce. At the outset, Quintilian says that the discussion fulfills his promise in Book II to examine not only the art and the artist, but the work of art itself. The position of the chapter results from following through this plan: Books III through XI have discussed the art, the earlier part of Book XII relates to the artist, and there now remains the oration itself. Some of the specific material in the chapter has been touched upon elsewhere in the *Institutio,* but not its basic theme, the possible varieties of style. Quintilian was quite right to emphasize it, for the vast system of rhetorical rules he has outlined only too easily might be taken to mean that there was a single uniform excellence, and, as we have seen, Quintilian did not believe this. The position of the discussion in the penultimate chapter of the work helps to show once again that oratory is a high art, not a mechanical science.

Quintilian's analysis of stylistic variation is principally concerned with two famous concepts found in many earlier writers: Atticism and the "characters" of style. The first implies a somewhat historical, the second a more critical approach. Neither topic as such has been discussed elsewhere in the *Institutio.*

Quintilian begins with the assertion that no single style will please everyone. Tastes differ in different times and places and among different individuals. He then proceeds to demonstrate this proposition by an analogy between rhetoric and the plastic arts, with a brief account of the history of painting and sculpture (XII,x,3–9). These passages are ultimately derived from Xenocrates and Antigonus, writers of the third century B.C., but discussions probably were also to be found in several more recent critics. There are somewhat similar historical surveys in the *Natural History* of the elder Pliny.[23] The comparison between the arts and oratory was probably a commonplace too; it appears briefly in Cicero,[24] and the twelfth oration of Dio Chrysostom, delivered in A.D. 97, contains a good comparison of poetry and sculpture. The point of the discussion in Quintilian is simply the variety of excellence among artists. The earliest are called crude, and some historical change is recognized, but Quintilian is not trying to demonstrate progress or decay. After the initial development there is variety in excellence. Certain virtues can hardly be combined, natural grace with awesome grandeur, for example. Among painters and sculptors, Quintilian does not grant clear superiority in all respects to any one artist, but when he turns to orators there is, of course, Cicero. Greek orators are not discussed here, but the characteristic virtues of the major Roman orators of the republic and empire are summarized (XII,x,10–11). Cicero alone has them all, but still falls short of perfection. Indeed, he has had many detractors, and this leads to the question of Atticism.

## II   *Atticism*

Quintilian's view of Atticism is essentially that of Cicero.[25] "Attic" originally meant simply the oratory of Attica, the district of Athens. In Asia Minor, however, the oratory was less polished and refined, and bombast much more to the popular taste. In contrast to the Asian style, the true variety of Attic oratory was forgotten, and later critics applied the term "Attic" only to the most extreme models of purity and simplicity, especially Lysias. Like Cicero, Quintilian regards this usage as historically unjustified and as esthetically constraining. If any one is to be taken as the finest Attic orator, he feels it should be the man with the greatest power, Demosthenes (XII,x, 23–24). Insofar as it relates to Atticism, Quintilian's account seems correct, though his picture of Asianism is somewhat superficial.

In the first century B.C. a neo-Atticist movement had flourished at Rome, led by Calvus and Brutus, cultivating a simple and pure, but dry and unrhythmical Latin style, and attacking Cicero as a veritable Asianist. It was in reply to Brutus that Cicero wrote his thoughts on Atticism, which he identified with varied and tasteful excellence. Quintilian goes a step beyond anything Cicero says in maintaining the fundamental inappropriateness of the spirit of neo-Atticism to the Latin language (XII,x,27–39). This is quite consistent with what he has said in Book X about the difficulty of writing Latin. According to Quintilian, Latin is less euphonious than Greek (for example, it lacks the sounds represented by zeta and upsilon, but has the ugly *f*, and many words end in a cow-like mooing)[26] and as compared to Greek it is deficient in vocabulary. The first point is rather subjective and certainly cannot be judged by a modern critic; the second point is indubitable. What is the implication of this situation for Latin style, Quintilian asks himself (XII,x,35); a logical point, apparently never before raised. His conclusion is that Roman writers must avoid incongruity between delicate thoughts and ugly words. "We cannot be so graceful; let us be stronger. We are inferior in subtlety; let us prevail by weight. The Greeks have an appropriate precision; let us beat them in fullness" (XII,x,36). It is thus obvious: the austerity of the Atticists is ineffective in Latin, the elegant purity at which they aimed cannot be achieved, and the fullness of the Ciceronian style is a more natural quality in great Roman oratory. If the material is inappropriate to elaboration, the thing to do is to imitate the method and judgment of Cicero in his private cases, or that of one of the earlier Roman orators whom Cicero had tried to present as equivalent to the Attic orators.

In Greek literature, where Atticism in the narrow sense was more possible and appropriate, it lasted for several centuries. Neo-Atticism in Latin is chiefly a phenomenon of the mid-first century B.C., but Quintilian says some few speakers in his time affected it (XII,x,14), and in most periods there were some writers who put especially high value on an austere Latinity. In arguing for Ciceronian fullness, Quintilian is not only opposing neo-Atticism, but dealing another blow at the declamatory style of Seneca's imitators, which, though it might be regarded as Asian in its bizarre affectations, was Atticist in avoiding long sentences, amplification, and rhythmical flow of words.

In the ensuing discussion (XII,x,40–48), Quintilian reveals that he also is opposing another critical position which has some practical similarities with Atticism, though it did not seek to imitate Greek models or to freeze linguistic usage at a particular historical stage. This was the view that expression should be entirely natural, resembling the language of everyday life, even vulgar if necessary, but avoiding all artificiality. Such a view originated with the Stoics, one of whose famous doctrines was that no word was in itself obscene.[27] Its appeal to some intellectuals of the first century A.D. can be seen in the novel-like *Satyricon* of Petronius, in which much of the vigor comes from the artistically selected, but frankly vulgar language and situation. Indeed, the vitality of all the satiric forms at Rome owed much to their natural language. Twentieth-century writers have similarly sought strength in casting off inhibitions. Throughout the *Institutio*, Quintilian has stressed natural expression, and he thus feels some sympathy with the naturalists, especially in contrast to the commoner declamatory style (XII,x,42), but he also feels that an absolute dependence on natural expression is inadequate for the purposes of great oratory, which is not simply to narrate, but to charm and to move. Nature herself has granted us additional aids to persuasion, there is variety in eloquence, and the best indication of whether a man speaks in accordance with nature is the effectiveness of his speech (XII,x,44). What is suitable will vary, not only from situation to situation, but from age to age. It is here that Cicero's deficiency in *sententiae* for the tastes of Quintilian's times is admitted.

Before turning to the characters of style, Quintilian inserts a digression on the proper relation between a delivered and a published speech (XII,x,49–57). This might logically have been put in Book X or XI, but was suggested at this point by the question whether the same style is appropriate in each case. It must be clearly understood that Quintilian is not discussing whether a different style is appropriate for oratory and for essays or other written composi- tions. He has already made it abundantly clear that different genres have different requirements. The question here is solely what kind of changes an orator should make in a speech between delivery and publication, and only one objective in publication is considered, the preservation of the speech as a model of oratory. This was certainly a common objective, though some speeches of Cicero and others were also published for political reasons. Quintilian's assumption is that if a particular speech is very effective it should be preserved as a work of art, and he does not favor trying to purify a speech of showy but popular passages to please austere critics.

Two exceptions are admitted. Sometimes in delivery a speech has to be shortened, but the whole may be published. This may be taken to approve the practice of Pliny who in the *Panegyricus* greatly am- plified the text between delivery and publication.[28] And some pas- sages introduced for the sake of particular judges may be cut out as unrepresentative of the orator's general artistic judgment. In Cicero's career the practical situations were sometimes more complicated than Quintilian allows for, but his advice was doubtless suitable for ordinary imperial oratory.

### III   *The Characters of Style*

Finally, Quintilian considers the three "characters" or kinds of style (XII,x,58–76), derived from Theophrastus, but principally de- veloped by rhetoricians of the first century B.C.[29] Accounts varied considerably from critic to critic. Quintilian's approach is naturally similar to that of Cicero.[30] He describes a plain style, a grand style, and an intermediate style which is florid and smooth, and these are associated with the three functions of the orator in instructing, stir- ring the emotions, and charming the mind. If only a single style were to be followed, it should be the grand, which is suitable for the greatest cases, but in fact Quintilian, like Cicero, rejects the idea of limiting stylistic variations to three patterns (XII,x,66). There are, rather, countless different possible styles from the plainest to the grandest, just as there are countless possible gradations in musical pitch or in the direction of the wind. Every possible style has its proper use. Furthermore, there often should be considerable varia- tion of style within a single speech, as the orator turns his attention to the proper function of the different parts and needs to conciliate, to instruct, or to move (XII,x,70).

A single orator will speak gravely, severely, sharply, violently, rapidly, verbosely, sarcastically, genially, informally, simply, pleasantly, gently, sweetly, briefly, or urbanely; he will not everywhere be like himself, but everywhere worthy of himself. (XII,x,71)

This is entirely sensible, for it allows for variety and art, and at the same time demands a standard of quality. It is often overlooked by critics, ancient and modern, who try to classify a single speech in a particular style; it is a rare speech which will not demand variety.

Quintilian winds up his remarks on stylistic variation with a parting blow at the corrupted style, immediately recognizable when compared with true eloquence. The perfect orator will do all things with ease, and he will do them with judgment. It is Quintilian's innermost conviction that in style, as in morality, what is good is immediately apprehended unless men have been corrupted by some unnatural and temporary aberration of taste. Excellence in all its variety manifests itself in practical effect: the army in devoted readiness, the assembly in rapt attention, the statesman resolved for action, the judge in tears.

# CHAPTER 6

## *The Final Picture*

THE objective of the rhetorical training which Quintilian sets forth is the creation of an orator variously called good, consummate, or perfect. The preface to Book I had described this ideal man briefly; Book XII examines him in greater detail.

At the beginning of the book, in an elaborately developed nautical metaphor, Quintilian expresses great nervousness about its projected contents. He is going to sail far beyond most rhetorical writers to seas traversed before only by Cicero, and will even go beyond Cicero. What he means is that he is going to discuss subjects not ordinarily part of rhetorical treatises and that the closest precedent is Cicero's *On the Orator*. It is rhetorically suitable for the last book to be introduced with a fanfare of amplification, but Quintilian is not quite so original as he implies. Almost all the topics had been discussed by earlier writers, but not necessarily in rhetorical treatises. Dialogues of Plato and Aristotle, Hellenistic discussions of philosophy and rhetoric, and works like Cicero's treatise *On Duties* related to some portions of the book. Monographs on art and style also made their contribution. On the other hand, no Roman writer puts quite so much emphasis on the moral character of the orator, and Quintilian may have been nervous about the criticism of contemporary orator-informers which this implies.[1] As far as the subject matter goes, however, Quintilian's originality, here as elsewhere, consists primarily of synthesis and evaluation of earlier discussions in the light of his own principles and experience and in terms of his resolve to view the orator as a whole.

The ideal orator in Quintilian's view is a man with great natural gifts who has acquired all the technical knowledge outlined in the *Institutio* and who also has built up a facility at using his knowledge. He must of course be an active, practicing orator, not primarily a declaimer or teacher. The preface to Book I had promised in Book

XII a discussion of the orator's character, his policy in undertaking and carrying on cases, his style, and his retirement. In the course of Book II this was revised into a promise to discuss not only the art of rhetoric, but the artist and the work of art, and at the end of that book the need to examine the artist's "instruments" was added. The actual discussion is unevenly carried out, but Book XII may be said to deal first with the orator's moral and intellectual qualities or "instruments," then with the development of his career, including the moral choices involved, with a chapter on the work of art inserted. The construction of the book has often been criticized and thought to show some of the haste of composition confessed in the letter to the bookseller Trypho prefixed to Book I.[2]

The moral assets of the orator are the most important, as the preface to Book I had already made clear. Cato's definition of an orator as a good man skilled in speaking is the basic concept, and Quintilian insists on the paradox that no man can be an orator in the full sense if he is not also a good man. The development of this idea had been carried on chiefly by the Stoics, but it is similar, as the reference to Cato shows, to the traditional Roman ideal, a man austerely moral, self-reliant, public spirited. Here Quintilian advances a number of arguments why only a good man can be a perfect orator (XII,i,1–13). The most interesting is perhaps the psychological argument that only the good man has adequate freedom from anxiety, cares, and passions to devote himself to the task. He alone is well adjusted, as we might say today. Furthermore, nothing is ideal if there is something better, and a good man is better than a bad man. And it is probable that the good man will be more consistently successful in presenting truth and honorable actions than will a clever man who does not believe in them.

A conspicuous feature of the discussion is the polarization of good and bad. A man is regarded as one or the other, as perfectly good or perfectly villainous. The possibility of men being mixtures of good and bad is not discussed, and in Quintilian's view there are apparently no faults which can exist in a man without somehow affecting his oratory. The position is Stoic, for the Stoics regarded all sins as equal, and if a man committed one he was as bad as if he had committed them all. The practicality of this view can be criticized, but it is logically valid if we remember that Quintilian is here not discussing orators in general, but thinking about some uniquely great orator, an ideal to be set in place of the philosopher king or the traditional sage. Of this man it is perfectly reasonable to require that he be lacking in no way.

Not only does Quintilian sharply separate good and bad men, but he believes that what is good is self-evident. It is the consensus of good men (I,vi,45). All the world can recognize an informer. At one time or other several qualities are mentioned which the good man will have, among them truth, honor, prudence, frugality, a love of praise, a sense of fairness. He will not be dishonest or shameful or stupid or selfish or envious or lustful. Subsequently, when talking about philosophy, Quintilian stresses the fact that the good orator must be within Roman traditions (XII,ii,7), and that is doubtless true here too. His moral qualities are to be those traditionally associated with the great Romans of the past. They are conventional virtues, but probably with a greater pride in worthy accomplishment than Christianity approved (XII,i,8), and with less value put on cleverness than Greeks had granted.

The orator has some special moral dilemmas. Must he always tell the literal truth? What is he to do if asked to defend a man he believes to be guilty? First of all, the orator may practice either side of an issue, since this exercise will give him a better understanding of the truth. Beyond that, the orator will sometimes defend a guilty man (XII,i,34), and in an earlier book it was implied that he will sometimes knowingly introduce false witnesses (V,vii,13), but in each case he must have a good moral reason for doing so. He will, for example, try to defend however he can a man accused of plotting against a tyrant, since any tyranny is wrong (XII,i,40). He will try to show that something was not done if he believes it was justly done, but knows that the judge will not accept that plea (XII,i,41). More than that, if he thinks a defendant will mend his ways, he will work for the man's acquittal (XII,i,42). One wonders what Domitian thought of all of this; he had in 91 executed a man for speaking against tyrants too pointedly.[3]

Quintilian's position here should be compared to Cicero's, although Quintilian does not make any specific reference. Cicero thought that an orator was justified in speaking in defense of a client even if guilty unless that client was particularly vicious or impious.[4] On the other hand, to undertake prosecution an orator must have compelling moral reasons. In a later discussion (XII,vii,1) Quintilian agrees with the second point. His differences with the first result from his taking a black and white view of everything. Cicero, who only claimed to discover probabilities, not the final truth, saw that there was hardly a defendant on whose behalf something could not justly be said, for men are guilty in various degrees: to him the function of the orator is to be a fair defender. Quintilian, on the other hand, more arrogantly expects the orator to prejudge his own client. The orator must decide whether the prospective client is morally or equitably entitled to win. As long as he decides in favor of the client, he is justified in doing everything possible in order to win, in extreme cases even using fraud, but if he should come to doubt his client, it is his duty to relinquish the case (XII,vii,6). Chapter vii discusses various matters which may figure in a patron's acceptance or rejection of cases, since he will probably not be able to accept all worthy cases offered him, but the fundamental question is always the patron's judgment of his client's moral position.

The first chapter of Book XII, in addition to discussing the morality of the orator, has something to say about the practicality of the ideal, but since this is resumed in the last chapter of the book it may be deferred while we look at the qualities in addition to virtue which the orator should have. These are a knowledge of philosophy, of law, and of historical and poetic example.

Quintilian's attitude toward philosophy is consistent throughout the work. He scorns contemporary philosophers; he finds the philosophical ideal lacking in civic virtues; philosophy can be feigned, eloquence cannot (XII,iii,12). But philosophy as discussed by the great philosophers of the past is necessary to an orator, and the split between philosophy and rhetoric should never have occurred in the first place. What the orator particularly needs is a knowledge of character and of the honorable and just, that is to say of ethics, but logic will contribute to the orator's argumentation, and natural philosophy, in which are included astronomy, physics, and metaphysics, will give nobility and profundity to eloquence, as well as provide some specific useful themes such as the role of providence in human affairs or the validity of augury and oracles.

As examples of the good effect of philosophy on oratory, Quintilian cites (XII,ii,22) the influence of Anaxagoras on Pericles and of Plato on Demosthenes, neither a very good example, since none of Pericles' speeches survived to be studied, and it is unlikely that Demosthenes actually studied with Plato. Cicero's debt to the Academy is mentioned also and is more real. Quintilian does not want his orator to be the follower of any one philosophical school; he should choose what is best from each (XII,ii,27). Though he criticizes the Stoics for neglect of eloquence (XII,i,25), it is clear throughout the *Institutio* that he is closer to them than to any other group. This was true in his definition of rhetoric, in his account of elementary education, and in his own moral position, particularly the view of men as good or bad just mentioned.

It is, however, a mistake to attribute Quintilian's theories to Stoic sources if the real sources are unknown, for he no more belongs to a philosophical than he does to a rhetorical school (III,i,22). His dislike of contemporary philosophy is consistent, as has been said, with the views of Vespasian and Domitian, but it is also consistent with his own character, and can hardly be labeled flattery. In the late first century A.D. the creative vitality of philosophy was at one of the lowest points in Western history, the primary reason being that the nature of man and the universe was widely regarded as being understood as well as could reasonably be expected. Little happened to challenge assumptions and awaken doubts or a sense of wonder in men's minds as long as the empire ground on along its apparently destined course.

The discussion of philosophy ends with a characteristic insistence on practical action. The Greeks are preeminent in moral precepts, but the Romans in what is more important, moral actions. Fortitude, justice, loyalty, self-control, frugality, indifference to pain or death can best be learned from Roman heroes like Fabricius, Curius, Regulus, Decius, and Mucius (XII,ii,30). The perfect orator should look for approval not so much to his immediate contemporaries as to posterity. As in the implied criticism of the informers and in the defense of the would-be tyrannicide, there is here a possible sign of dissatisfaction with certain prevailing conditions which we have not found elsewhere in Quintilian. Book XII, the last Quintilian wrote, begins to show the strain of the end of Domitian's reign.

The remaining "instruments" are next discussed. Quintilian is appalled at an orator who has to turn continually to someone else, even during a trial, for legal advice (XII,iii,1–3). The greatest Roman orators, like Cato and Cicero, combined legal knowledge with eloquence, and the ideal orator will too. This is represented as not very difficult: most legal experts are said to be those who have failed as orators (XII,iii,9). The final instrument is the knowledge of examples from history or poetry, rather briefly and superficially treated (XII,iv). The description of the orator is then concluded in a short chapter (XII,v) on the need for self-assurance and physical assets, especially a strong voice. This seems oddly placed here, as though Quintilian felt these points had not been adequately stressed, but did not want to take the trouble to rewrite other portions of the work. He was hurrying toward publication.

In what is now the sixth chapter Quintilian turns to a survey of the perfect orator's active career, taking him from his first appearance at the bar through his retirement, discussed in the eleventh chapter. As in the educational discussions of Books I and II, actual age is not a consideration. In Quintilian's opinion the orator should not begin to appear in the law courts until he is well trained, but he must not put off speaking until he has lost his youthful nerve (XII, vi,2–3). To judge from the examples he cites, Quintilian regarded the early twenties as the most suitable time for most men to start. He does not refer to his own career, but he was probably about twenty when he went back to Spain to practice. Naturally, the first case should be a simple and favorable one if possible. To us it would seem reasonable that a young man should begin to plead as a junior collaborator with some experienced orator, and there was nothing in the Roman system to prevent this, but the famous orators at Rome often began with some brash prosecution of their own or with a case in which they were personally involved. The young orator is urged to follow Cicero's example of taking leave from the bar after a little practical experience, as soon as he knows what is really involved in his career, in order to perfect himself by further study (XII,vi,6).

The next question is what cases are to be taken, a subject already touched upon from the moral viewpoint. Defense is agreed to be the more congenial, but prosecution is sometimes a duty. The perfect orator will refuse to indulge ambition by selling his services to the powerful against the humble, or to seek notoriety by attacking the influential without provocation. He will not charge fees in proportion to the seriousness of the case, but there is nothing wrong in accepting enough money to support oneself in return for honorable service (XII,vii,9). Earning money at Rome was always undignified, and from the end of the third century B.C. until the mid-first century A.D. payment of pleaders was illegal. The law, however, was often flouted, and the emperor Claudius finally legalized direct payments.[5]

Quintilian's orator must study his case carefully, preferably interviewing personally those involved, allowing them to tell their stories in their own way, while taking notes (XII,viii,7–8). The litigant himself should be made to go over his version several times, as new details are apt to appear and clients often lie to their own patrons.

Well they might if they thought he would abandon their case if he decided them to be guilty! Documents must be examined personally and carefully, for they often will not be quite as alleged (XII,viii,12). Then, the patron should pretend to be the opposing orator and cross-examine his client mercilessly (XII,viii,10). And finally he should assume the role of judge and examine the effect of his own case (XII,viii,15). All this is practical and shows Quintilian's own experience and methodical approach. In the actual trial (XII,ix) the orator must always keep the case and his client's interests uppermost in his mind, not seeking applause, or scorning small matters, or indulging rancor and heaping insults on the opponent. He will keep to what he has written if possible, but will know the case so well and listen so carefully to the opponent that he will be able to improvise if necessary.

It is at this point that the lengthy chapter on the speech as a work of art and the orator's style is inserted, after which Quintilian returns to his survey of the orator's career. The perfect orator has grown old in his eloquent service. He must himself watch the signs of lessening physical powers of voice and endurance and, unlike Domitius Afer, voluntarily seek retirement before his effectiveness falls off (XII,xi,1–3). His service to society is by no means at an end, for he will write history or law or a treatise on oratory or moral philosophy, and his house will continue to be a resort for the new generation of orators seeking his advice and criticism (XII,xi,4–5).

Here at last Quintilian has completed his intended work; the orator's primary, secondary, and adult levels of education have all been examined, and the promises of the preface of Book I fulfilled. At the very end (XII,xi,8–31) he adds some intensely felt concluding sections on the practicality of his ideal, designed to prove that what he has demanded, not only grammar and rhetoric, but ethics and law, is not beyond achievement. The words seem chiefly addressed to students, but perhaps also to other teachers.

To prove that the goal is practical, Quintilian advances several arguments: the natural powers of the human mind for greatness and goodness are immense; will power and motivation are important factors, "for nature produced us for the sake of superior intelligence" (XII,xi,12); since it should be easier to live in accordance with nature than against her, it should be possible to fulfill human potential. Further, there is time enough to learn what is important if order and reason and the mean prevail, if teachers do not hold us back, if we do not become so fond of declamation that we never get to the law courts, if we do not think we must read every book ever written, if we do not waste time in the trivial amenities of social life.

It is interesting to see that Roman educators of the first century, like modern educators, were concerned with what is now called the knowledge explosion. Quintilian's attitude, that one cannot learn everything, but can, with a sense of proportion and clarity of goal, learn what counts, is still valid. He cites examples of great minds of the past to show what can be done; look at Hippias, Gorgias, Plato, Aristotle, Cato, Varro, Cicero, and more recently at Celsus, whom Quintilian has repeatedly referred to as a writer on rhetoric, "a man of no extraordinary ability," who yet succeeded in writing an encyclopedia. "Antiquity has furnished us with so many teachers, so many examples, that no age is happier in its historical setting than ours for whose education previous ages have labored" (XII,xi,22). Finally, there is no natural law that says the best is past (XII,xi,25). Quintilian here again rejects the hypothesis of irresistible literary decline which some of his contemporaries found compelling. And even if a particular individual cannot be the greatest that has ever been, the second rank is a worthy one; it is worth while to aim as high as possible.

Therefore, let us seek with all our heart that very majesty of speech, the immortal gods' finest gift to man, and without which all creatures are mute and lack both present glory and the memory of posterity, and let us strive always for the best, for in doing it, we will either emerge at the summit or at least see many beneath us. (XII,xi,30)

This love of speech, this driving sense of the need for effort, this challenge of ambition are the fundamental instincts of Quintilian in his own career and constitute the philosophy which he tried to teach to others.

## I  The Feasibility of Quintilian's Ideal

When Quintilian considers the practicality of the oratorical ideal, he is solely concerned with showing his contemporaries that they should not be put off by its difficulty. A critic with the benefit of historical perspective is obliged to ask various other questions about that ideal. Was it a feasible one for Quintilian's age, that is, not just a possible one, but a suitable one? What would the ideal orator in fact accomplish? And then, did Quintilian's ideal bear fruit? Did anyone try to accomplish what he described? Or to put it another way, what was Quintilian's impact on his own or succeeding periods at Rome?

The conditions of Quintilian's time would seem to have put two kinds of limitation on the ideal orator: political activity under an emperor like Domitian was unfeasible and the philosophical environment was sterile. In both ways Cicero had been presented with challenging opportunities which Quintilian's orator could not normally be expected to encounter. Quintilian of course might privately reply that he hoped the conditions of the later part of Domitian's reign would not prove normal, but the structure of the empire certainly had to be viewed as the status quo. Furthermore, he might say that a perfectly ideal orator would be able to bend the emperor and all the state to his noble purposes, and that under the conditions of empire there was a peculiar opportunity waiting to be achieved, however unlikely success seemed in contemporary fact. The advising of the emperor is occasionally referred to as a function of the orator, and Seneca could reasonably be regarded as having played this role with the young Nero, thus achieving some influence on the course of events. There is one passage which develops somewhat more clearly the functions of the perfect orator:

For we are not training some public hireling or a voice motivated by pay or even, to avoid harsher terms, a competent enough advocate in litigation commonly known as a pleader [*causidicus*], but a man both outstanding in natural ability and deeply learned in all the fairest arts, in short, a gift of providence to human life, of the sort which no previous age has known, unique and perfect in everything, perceiving what is best, speaking as is best. How small a part of this man's work will be the defense of the innocent or the suppression of the crimes of the wicked or the support of truth against fraud in financial cases? Our ideal orator will take part in these activities too, but he will shine more glorious in greater matters when the deliberations of the senate are to be directed and mistaken public opinion is to be led toward a better goal. (XII,i,25–26)

This is an unusual passage. Throughout most of the *Institutio* Quintilian is thinking about judicial oratory. Of course he is usually also thinking about average orators and not the perfect orator. Here the perfect orator emerges and would seem to be primarily a public spokesman for the emperor, as for example Trachalus, whom Quintilian admired (X,i,119), had been for Otho.[6] But the passage continues with a famous quotation from Virgil, the lines in the first *Aeneid* in which Neptune is compared to a statesman, calm in civil discord. In this passage Virgil certainly had in mind the emperor Augustus as bringer of peace after civil war. Quintilian then pictures the orator in time of war, inspiring his troops before battle. These military and civic functions in practice were combined only in the person of an emperor or a caesar, and in the final analysis Quintilian's orator, the best man in the state, should be the emperor or his heir, an orator-king.

But to suggest this openly was not possible under the suspicious Domitian. Even though in theory the principate was conferred by the senate on the first man of the state, the most Quintilian could actually hope for was the training of one of his pupils, Domitian's heir, into a perfect orator. One thinks of Plato's efforts to educate Dionysius or of Quintilian's own picture in Book I of Aristotle teaching Alexander the Great. The result seems to be that we should distinguish Quintilian's remarks on the opportunity open to an ideal orator from the opportunities open to oratory in general. It is the latter which is the subject of Tacitus' *Dialogue* and other discussions of the time. The general opportunities were limited and unencouraging and Quintilian does not discuss them. The theoretical opportunities were enormous and staggering; they had been approached perhaps by Seneca and by Trachalus, they might be regarded as a goal in the education of a prince, and they were just within the realm of possible imagination. Quintilian does not demand more than that.

## II  *The Second Sophistic*

Quintilian's own philosophic imagination was limited, but he seems to have felt at least the theoretical possibility of something special being achieved by a philosophical orator. After lamenting the split between rhetoric and philosophy, he goes on to say:

O that the time may come when some perfect orator whom we desire will claim as his own this art which has become hated because of its arrogant name and the vices of those who corrupt its benefits, and will bring it back into the body of eloquence as though recovering stolen property! (XII,2,9–10)

There exists, therefore, to his mind at least, some remote opportunity for philosophical oratory. In the Greek world at this very time a literary movement was gaining new strength which, though often superficial and empty, aimed at fulfilling some of the functions of

Quintilian's ideal orator, including the advising of princes and cities and the eloquent expression of moral philosophy in popular terms. This movement is what is called the second sophistic.[7] It was modeled to some extent on the epideictic oratory of Greek sophists like Gorgias, Prodicus, and Isocrates. Its practitioners usually began as teachers of rhetoric or advocates in law courts, especially in the cities of Asia Minor. Acquiring some reputation, they traveled around the Greek world to the major cities and festivals giving exhibitions of their skill at speaking and, in the case of the better ones, usually seeking to recommend some philosophical or cultural views. The most successful eventually reached Rome itself. The high point of the second sophistic was the reign of Hadrian in the second century, but it was already well underway in Quintilian's time and he certainly knew and probably had heard its leading practitioners. In the same breath, his own pupil Pliny mentions studying with Quintilian and listening to the great sophist Nicetus.[8]

Of all the sophists of the Flavian period, the one we know best is Dio of Prusa, called Chrysostom, or "the golden tongued," whose views on reading and dictation have already been mentioned. His career will serve to illustrate the situation of sophistic oratory in Quintilian's time. Dio was born about the same time as Quintilian, though at the opposite end of the empire, and according to the essay on him by Synesius was originally a pure sophist, delivering such speeches as an encomium of hair to show his own cleverness, and criticizing the philosophers much as Quintilian does, though perhaps more violently.

After coming to Rome from Asia early in Vespasian's reign, Dio seems to have been converted to Stoicism, possibly by Musonius Rufus, who was exempted from Vespasian's anti-philosophical edict,[9] and though he continued to give great attention to style and form throughout his life and to use oratory as the vehicle of his thought, his orations take on a more serious purpose. In A.D. 82 he was involved in the downfall of Flavius Sabinus, Domitian's cousin, and exiled by Domitian for life both from Italy and his native Bithynia.[10] As a result, he adopted the way of life of a cynic philosopher, giving up all worldly possessions except a copy of the *Phaedo* of Plato and Demosthenes' speech *On the False Embassy*, and wandering around, chiefly along the Danube frontier, speaking to anyone who would listen. With the assassination of Domitian in A.D. 96 he returned to a more comfortable life and the company of the great, delivering four speeches on kingship before the Emperor Trajan, speaking at the Olympic games, and taking part in the life of his home town, where Pliny as governor encountered him.[11]

Though Domitian probably had regarded Dio as a disloyal critic, his attitude toward the state as seen in his extant speeches is loyal and constructive. The speeches before Trajan show respect, but not undue flattery, and the model of the Homeric king as interpreted by the Stoics is presented to the emperor for his imitation. Dio's life as a cynic resulted from the need to make the best of circumstances, not from a fundamental cynicism, and his Stoicism is a moderate one too, consonant with Roman traditions. His speeches are full, but gracefully expressed, generally lacking in pomposity or excessive artificiality. His models were Attic, but his language is that of his age. His words, like his career, appear sincere, cultivated, well-intentioned. There is little or no absolute originality in what he says, but a good deal of re-expression of the tradition of Hellenism. His worst quality is perhaps a tendency to make everything too obvious, too explicit. What might have been effective if subtly expressed seems trite and trivial by being over developed, an example being his telling of the story of the choice of Heracles in the first oration on kingship.

From the perspective of modern times there seems to be a great deal about Dio that Quintilian could have approved. He would of course have disagreed with Dio on small points, like the use of dictation, but that is trivial. He almost certainly knew Dio in the years before 82, when both were prominent in the intellectual life of the capital. He could not mention Dio in the *Institutio* without incurring Domitian's wrath, nor did he live to see or hear Dio after exile when his greatest speeches were delivered, and certainly he does not have him in mind as an example of what may be accomplished. Furthermore, Quintilian is seeking a Roman orator and probably would have viewed a *contemporary* Greek as an unlikely vessel of genius. But as has been said, Dio is not the only sophist, not even the only philosophical sophist. He is just one whom we happen to know well from this particular time. What we need to conclude is that Quintilian's concept of the good orator, derived from other sources, was shared by contemporary Greeks who were in fact trying to put it into effect. Roman oratory on the other hand was much more limited: it consisted chiefly of the practical oratory of the law courts and senate and of declamation, which rarely attempted anything in the grand sophistic tradition, but was devoted to *suasoriae* and *controversiae*, ostensibly the more practical forms. These limitations result partly from the practical and rather narrow character of the Romans, partly from the fact that an oratorically ambitious Roman did at least have a few significant practical opportunities still open to him. Both nations agreed in putting a very high value on eloquence.

Quintilian's ideal orator then might be described as the achievement by a Roman, within Roman traditions, and thus without the shame of a wandering cynic, of something analogous to the oratorical, philosophical, political, and cultural goals of a Greek sophist. The orator will of course be a practical man, ready to appear in the law courts and to hold office, but this was true also of many Greek sophists like Dio in their own cities. The scale of responsibility rather than the nature of the duties will differ, and both orators will advise kings and great assemblies. The question we must ask then is whether Quintilian's ideal, perhaps shared by some others and taught to his own pupils, received any kind of Roman expression. Does the second sophistic have a Roman counterpart?

### III  *Pliny and Fronto*

It does, but only in a limited way, in the efforts of Pliny and Fronto, and probably others like them. Pliny was Quintilian's pupil, perhaps his greatest pupil, though we must not conclude that Quintilian fancied Pliny the potential perfect orator or that Pliny regarded himself as the serious rival of Cicero. Pliny shared Quintilian's values in being a practicing orator, not a declaimer, and one with ambition to be truly eloquent; in feeling a duty to take his part in public life and serve the state; in having rather little interest in formal philosophy, but a strong moral sense; in a fondness for reading and an appreciation of the classics, but without despair at the state of letters in his own age; in cultivating a literary style which was contemporary and flexible, but belonged to the tradition of Cicero rather than that of Sallust or of Seneca.[12] As a member of a younger generation Pliny's tastes are not exactly those of Quintilian, of course, and in a few specific ways he departs from Quintilian's advice, for example, in the fact that his one surviving speech does not quite follow the structure recommended by Quintilian.

This speech is the *Panegyric,* an elaborated version of the speech of thanks which Pliny addressed to Trajan in the Roman senate as he assumed the consulship for two months in the fall of A.D. 100. When read superficially, the *Panegyric* seems only a tiresome list of Trajan's virtues, but on further examination it becomes clear that Pliny is not currying favor with the emperor, but painstakingly setting out Trajan's conduct as a precedent for future emperors. To the minds of many senators, Trajan was the first emperor who had behaved as an emperor should, and if his example could be canonized, a considerable constitutional gain would be made. Pliny's function then is a political one, worthy of Quintilian's orator, and like the better Greek sophists he is using epideictic for a significant purpose. On the other hand, the literary achievement is not great, considerably inferior to Dio's address to Trajan a few years later. Pliny's tone is absolutely homogeneous: an exalted sincerity, adorned with constant *sententiae*. The variety characteristic of Cicero or even of Dio is lacking, no part is more passionate than any other, and there are no flights of fancy. If we regard the speech as a combined product of Roman laudations, as seen, for example, in funeral orations, and of Greek epideictic, it is clear that the Roman influence has won out.

Fronto, like Pliny, had a successful political career and held the consulship for two months in A.D. 143. He practiced in the courts and spoke often in the senate, but unlike Pliny he acquired a reputation as a rhetorician and played somewhat the role under the Antonines that Quintilian had played under the Flavians, being appointed tutor to Marcus Aurelius and Lucius Verus. Marcus at the time was already eighteen and Fronto never instructed him, or probably anybody else, in rhetorical theory, not to say grammar, but directed his reading and composition. We know Fronto from his correspondence with Marcus and others in the imperial circle. His chief concerns were with diction and figures, and with trying to keep Marcus from being converted to philosophy, in which he failed. He seems to have delighted in sophistic oratory, but of a very empty sort: the praise of dust or of negligence, or a Greek imitation of the speeches in Plato's *Phaedrus*. He never attained anything like the sense of purpose and influence demanded by Quintilian or the orator. Fronto doubtless knew Quintilian's *Institutio*, and occasionally may have in mind something Quintilian had said, but he never mentions him by name.

## IV  Quintilian and Tacitus

The second century A.D. was a generally happy time in Rome, and produced some of her greatest rulers. There was considerable freedom of speech, and much interest in literature, but the orator for whom Quintilian longed did not come. Tacitus proved a better prophet than Quintilian. We have already had occasion to mention his *Dialogue on the Orators,* and its relationship to Quintilian has been the subject of a number of studies.[13] Tacitus begins with the statement that the age is lacking in eloquence and that the name of orator scarcely survives, and he proceeds to report a discussion among three famous Romans as to why this is the case. The dramatic date is about A.D. 75, and Tacitus says that he himself was present, "still a young man." This suggests that publication occurred a considerable time later. One of the participants, Aper, does not accept the premise of the decline of oratory, but Tacitus himself clearly does, since he both begins and ends on this note and allows one of the other characters to state that even Aper does not believe the doctrine which he supports.[14]

Not only is the eloquence of the age of Vespasian given a low value, but contemporary rhetorical schools are derided too, with no hint that there might be exceptions.[15] Quintilian criticized much about oratory and education in the time of Vespasian, but felt that there had been some improvement subsequently; the view of Tacitus, however, would seem to be that Quintilian's school, which had been open several years at the time of the dialogue and even longer at the time of publication, had had no effect and could have no effect. This is bad enough as a criticism of Quintilian. It becomes an even more pointed criticism if the *Dialogue,* instead of being published a few years after the conversation it reports, actually dates from the reign of Nerva or Trajan, and the most learned and assured critics of Tacitus now seem virtually unanimous that this was the case.[16] First of all, it was the general custom, followed by Cicero in large part and by Quintilian, to avoid mention of living persons in literary discussions. Some of those in the *Dialogue* appear to have survived until the reign of Domitian. Yet sections of the work would have been rather dangerous to publish under Domitian, and Tacitus elsewhere implies that he published nothing throughout his reign.[17] The *Dialogue* is addressed to Fabius Julius, and a suitable time for addressing him would have been his consulship in A.D. 102. The return of relative freedom of speech after Domitian's assassination can be imagined to have raised expectations of the revival of eloquence, which all men of learning revered. But after five years had passed, rather little improvement was evident. What Tacitus seems to say is that eloquence was not temporarily suppressed by autocracy, but that the whole imperial system had produced order in the state so that not only opportunity, but even need for great oratory was gone. This had considerable point under Nerva and Trajan, and becomes more significant if one remembers that Tacitus, who had earned a reputation as an orator, apparently gave up the art and turned to historical composition during these years, much as Maternus in the *Dialogue* has given up oratory for poetry, and in a similarly critical mood.

There are a number of similarities between the *Dialogue* and the *Institutio*, resulting chiefly from the fact that they both deal with aspects of the historical condition of oratory at the same period. The later writer, and he is probably Tacitus as we have seen, should have known the earlier, but neither work is explicable primarily as an answer to the other. The *Dialogue*, for example, does not touch upon the most idealistic aspects of Quintilian's orator as an adviser to states and emperors and as an interpreter of philosophy, nor does it recognize Quintilian's ideas about education. It is likely that Tacitus simply chose to ignore what Quintilian had said as irrelevant, or as the view of a Flavian partisan.

Whatever the relationship between the two works, there are a number of points in the *Dialogue* which cast an interesting light on views of Quintilian. This is especially true of the matter of informers. Aper in the *Dialogue* asserts that not only could there be great oratory, but that able orators were living. With this Quintilian of course agreed. The examples Aper cites, however, are people whom Tacitus elsewhere identifies as more or less notorious informers, and the oratory described as that in vogue is the untrained, mercurial manner of informers.[18] Now Quintilian speaks of informers with disapproval and his insistence on the necessity of morality in oratory and the need for a thorough academic training perhaps results from his observation of contemporary conditions, but he avoids any direct discussion of the subject, he speaks sympathetically of a few orators whom Tacitus brands as informers, most notably Domitius Afer, and in general he supports the status quo. Possibly, like some of the emperors, he thought informers a regrettable necessity: one had to have them, but one didn't have to be one. His own early retirement and the one or two remarks we noted in Book XII may reveal a disillusion with Domitian, but this is apt to have resulted from the emperor's own increasing suspicions and cruelties, not from the activities of others. The informers flourished, but they had done so more or less consistently throughout Quintilian's life.

Tacitus' attitudes are rather extreme and embittered, but his picture of informers is generally confirmed by Pliny, Suetonius, Juvenal, and others. Thus Quintilian seems something of a Polyanna about Flavian oratory. If his assessment of contemporary conditions was too favorable, it was only too likely that his hopes for future developments would prove unrealistic. Flavian bias, optimism, and a certain vagueness about details are not inconsistent with the picture of Quintilian which has otherwise emerged.

## V  *Quintilian's Later Influence*

The history of Quintilian's subsequent reputation and influence makes an interesting study, for few classical authors have suffered such changes in fame.[19] In the generation after his death he was mentioned with respect by Pliny,[20] as we have seen, and cited by Juvenal,[21] possibly also a pupil, as an example of sobriety and of worldly success unusual in the teaching profession. Suetonius included a biography of him in his work on famous rhetoricians, but the discussion is now lost.[22] The impression we get is chiefly that Quintilian was a famous man, not that the *Institutio* was much read or that Quintilian's ideas were influential. As a matter of fact, the works most associated with his name were probably the two collections of declamations. In the third century, an unsuccessful claimant to the throne named Postumus is said to have been so eloquent that his declamations were inserted among those of Quintilian.[23]

From the late third to the fifth century A.D., Quintilian, like other classical authors, experienced a renaissance. In this age a kind of statesman-orator again emerged into prominence,[24] but it was Quintilian's writing on education and rhetoric that was best known, not his concept of the perfect orator. Indeed, Quintilian's fundamental theme and objective have had little or no influence on the history of Western thought, whereas his views on education and his rhetorical teachings have. In late antiquity, Jerome is the best example of a writer influenced by Quintilian's educational theories, especially in *Letter* CVII, which outlines a program for training a Christian girl, and is quite obviously adapted from Quintilian, though it does not mention his name. Among rhetoricians of later antiquity, there is perhaps less reference to Quintilian than might be expected, but the treatise of Julius Victor, dating from the fourth century, is heavily dependent on the *Institutio*. Cassiodorus in the sixth century, and Isidore of Seville in the seventh, drew on Quintilian and helped make him known indirectly to many medieval readers.

Direct knowledge of Quintilian's work declined in the early Middle Ages, and from the ninth century on only a mutilated text of the *Institutio* was generally available.[25] This text lacked the beginning of Book I, the end of Book V, all of Books VI and VII, much of Books VIII and IX, almost all the first chapter of Book X, portions of XI, and the end of XII. Though the general tenor of the work was clear from what survived, many of the most interesting sections were gone. Presumably the incomplete manuscripts were all derived from a single manuscript which had become unbound and lost whole gatherings.

Despite the fragmentary state of their text, Quintilian experienced a remarkable increase in fame among the Italian humanists of the fourteenth century. Perhaps they saw in him a counterpart of themselves, a literate enthusiast who looked back at all of classical letters as a source of education and inspiration. Petrarch addressed to Quintilian one of his letters to the dead in which he says that judging from the declamations, he had thought Quintilian over-rated, but then at last he had secured the *Institutio*, and fragmentary as it was, he came to understand from it Quintilian's greatness, which consists not in being, but in forming an orator.

All this time there were several complete manuscripts of the *Institutio* in central Europe. The first Italian humanist to discover one was Poggio, who in 1416, in a foul and forgotten dungeon in St. Gall, to his ineffable joy, discovered a complete text, full of dirt and covered with dust, but legible. The rediscovery of an ancient author was perhaps never greeted with such enthusiasm throughout the learned world, and Quintilian provided the inspiration for a new humanistic philosophy of education. For two hundred years he ranked in the eyes of many educated men all over Europe as one of the giants of Latin literature, worthy to be mentioned side by side with Virgil and Cicero. Among the writers who were impressed by Quintilian and adapted various aspects of his educational ideas were Pope Pius II, Guarino, Vegio, and Palmieri. Lorenzo Valla's extravagant love of Quintilian went so far that it offended the more staunch Ciceronians. In the fifteenth and sixteenth centuries this enthusiasm spread to northern Europe, where it was particularly manifest in the work of Rudolph Agricola and Erasmus, while Luther claimed that he preferred Quintilian to almost all authors, "in that he educates and at the same time demonstrates eloquence, that is, he teaches in word and in deed most happily."[26]

This is the high point of Quintilian's reputation as an educator. In the following centuries, he is often mentioned by writers like Montaigne and Lessing, and in England was praised by Pope and by

John Stuart Mill, but he made no major contribution to intellectual history, and by the late nineteenth century he seemed to be almost a neglected author, rather little read and rarely edited. He was never so popular in England as on the Continent. There have been only four reasonably complete English translations, one by W. Guthrie in 1756, one by J. Patsall in 1774, one by J. S. Watson in 1856, and one by H. E. Butler, in 1921. Watson's is by all odds the best; Butler's is the most easily available, but is filled with inaccuracies and infelicities.

In the mid-twentieth century Quintilian enjoys a secure place in the history of education, chiefly as the earliest spokesman for a child-centered education in which learning through play, treating children as human beings, and special concern for the early years of school are the dominant features. To students of speech and rhetoric, a not inconsiderable group in the United States, Quintilian is important for the fullness of the rhetorical system which he expounds. To the classicist, he is a good example of an intellectual of the Roman empire. And to all men he is a human being, caught between suffering and success.

# Notes and References

## Chapter One

1. For more extensive discussion of the nature and history of rhetoric, see George Kennedy, *The Art of Persuasion in Greece* (Princeton, 1963).

2. Though the State might regulate education, teachers were apt to be paid out of foundations privately established. See H. I. Marrou, *A History of Education in Antiquity* (London, 1956), pp. 102–105.

3. See M. L. Clarke, *Rhetoric at Rome* (London, 1953).

4. See S. F. Bonner, *Roman Declamation* (Liverpool and Berkeley, 1949).

5. *Professors of Bordeaux* (V),i,7. Most information in later writers about Quintilian's career is derived from Suetonius' *On Grammarians and Rhetoricians*. The index of that work lists Quintilian as the subject of a chapter, but the chapter is now lost.

6. *Controversiae* X,*pr.*,2 and X,iv,19.

7. According to the Scholiast on Juvenal VI,452, Quintilian studied with the grammarian Remmius Palaemon, in which case he probably was in Rome earlier. Quintilian's references to his own education in I,ii,23–24 and to Palaemon in I,iv,30 do not indicate any connection, but Quintilian may have come to disapprove of Palaemon's character, which was infamous; see Suetonius, *On Grammarians* 23.

8. Quintilian says he was an *adulescens* at the time, VI,i,14. For the date see Tacitus, *Annals* XIII,32.

9. See X,i,102 and Tacitus, *Annals* XIV,19.

10. X,v,19 and XII,xi,6. On the custom see Tacitus, *Dialogue on Orators* 34.

11. *Epistles* II,xiv,10.

12. I*J*,iv,31. In I*J*,iv,142 Quintilian seems to be developing the same view.

13. *Annals* IX,52; IV,66, and XIV, 19. Dio Cassius LIX,19.

14. VI,iii,68: "do *something* for the sake of your country."

15. *Galba* 4. On Spain in Quintilian's time, see R. Knox McElderry, "Vespasian's Reconstruction of Spain," *Journal of Roman Studies*, VIII (1918), 53–102.

16. *Galba* 10.

17. Some older editions and translations mistakenly refer to a Galba in VI,iii, but the name should be Gabba, a famous Augustan wit.

18. Suetonius, *Vespasian* 10, vouches for judicial disruptions.

19. *Ibid.*, 18.

20. See M. St.A. Woodside, "Vespasian's Patronage of Education and the Arts," *Transactions of the American Philological Association*, LXXIII (1942), 123–29.

21. Suetonius, *On Grammarians* 23. See R. P. Robinson, "The Roman Schoolteacher and his Reward," *Classical Weekly*, XV (1921), 57–61.

22. *Epistles* II,xiv,9 and VI,vi,3. Another possible pupil is Juvenal.

23. In VII,ii,5 he mentions "some

cases" involving identity which he had handled.

24. Dio Cassius LXV,15 and LXVI, 18.

25. Acts 25:23.

26. The date can be determined thus: Quintilian was writing the *Institutio* between A.D. 92 and 94, as is shown below. In the middle of this period, i.e., about 93, his elder son died at the age of about ten; at least he is said to have shown promise at nine and to have been sick for eight months before his death (VI,*pr.*,10). This son was thus born about 83. Quintilian's younger son died at the age of five while Quintilian was writing *De Causis* (VI,*pr.*,3 and 6). Since both sons were born before their mother was nineteen, it is unlikely that there was more than a year between them. Thus the younger son was born around 84 and died around 89, and the *De Causis* was written around 89.

27. *Controversiae* I,*pr.*,7.

28. *Satyricon* 1–4.

29. *Satires* VII,188–189. Quintilian's own words in VIII,iii,9–10, if taken literally, suggest that he owned a handsome grove of olive trees, but his use of the first person is perhaps rhetorical rather than personal.

30. *Epigrams* II,90.

31. Similar are *Epigrams* I,55 and II,53, whereas opposed sentiments are found in I,76 and V,56.

32. See, e.g., Martial I,25 and Pliny, *Epistles* I,1; II,10; V,10; IX,1.

33. I,*pr.*,6; IV,*pr.*,1; VI,*pr.*,1; XII, vi,31. His full name was probably M. Vitorius Marcellus, the reversal of *nomen* and *cognomen* being common in the empire.

34. Aulus Gellius IV,vii,1.

35. *On Grammarians* 24.

36. *Thebaid* XII,815.

37. *Silvae* II,7.

38. *Argonautica* I,15. On the date, see Ronald Syme, "The *Argonautica* of Valerius Flaccus, *Classical Quarterly,*

XXIII (1929), 129–137.

39. *Epigrams* IX,34.

40. Ausonius, *Speech of Thanks* (XX),7.

41. Dio Cassius LXVII,14.

42. For an instance of the latter, see Tacitus, *Histories,* IV,4.

43. *Domitian* 15.

44. In the Cabinet de France; see H. Cohen, *Descriptions historiques des monnaies frappées sous l'Empire romaines* (Paris, 1880), I, 539.

45. The identity of these people is unknown.

46. *Epistles* VI,32.

## Chapter Two

1. *Libri Ad Marcellum de Institutione Oratoria* as given there would be the full formal title. Some MSS give *De Institutione Oratoria,* but *Institutionis Oratoriae Libri,* which may be regarded as a shortened version, is the commoner title in later times. Two important MSS (Bg and Bn) have the plural, *Institutiones* (thus, in English, Quintilian's *Institutes*). The use of the form with *De* is supported by the example of the *De Causis* and Cicero's *De Oratore,* which is Quintilian's major inspiration.

2. See the usage in I,i,21 and I,ii,6.

3. See, e.g., I,*pr.*,21; I,xii,19; VII,iv, 28.

4. In III,iv,12 Quintilian follows the judgment of the majority. On the Theodoreans and Apollodoreans, see G. M. A. Grube, "Theodorus of Gadara," *American Journal of Philology,* LXXX (1959), 337–65.

5. See *Epistles* III,5.

6. The only other thing we know about Pliny's treatise is that it discussed declamation and gave examples of arguments, see Aulus Gellius IX,16.

7. See J. Morr, "Poseidonius von Rhodos über Dichtung und Redekunst," *Wiener Studien,* XLV (1926), 47; F. H. Colson, *M. Fabii Quintiliani Institutionis Oratoriae Liber I* (Cambridge, Eng., 1924), p. 6; Jean Cousin,

*Études sur Quintilien* (Paris, 1936), I, 638; Alain Michel, *Rhétorique et philosophie chez Cicéron. Essai sur les fondements philosophiques de l'art de persuader* (Paris, 1960), pp. 15–17.

8. *On the Orator* III,60; *Brutus*, 31.

9. For Vespasian in A.D. 71, the year of Quintilian's appointment see Dio Cassius LXV,13, and for Domitian on several occasions, but especially towards the end of his reign at the very time Quintilian was writing and publishing the *Institutio*, see Aulus Gellius XV,11. See the *Cambridge Ancient History* (Cambridge, Eng., 1936), XI, 9; 27; 31.

10. See E. Norden, "Die Composition and Litteraturgattung der Horazischen *Epistula ad Pisones*," *Hermes*, XL (1905), 481–528, which overstates the matter; Cousin (*op. cit. supra*, n.7), I,772; C. O. Brink, *Horace on Poetry: Prolegomena to the Literary Epistles* (Cambridge, Eng., 1963), pp. 20–24.

11. See R. G. Austin, *Quintiliani Institutionis Oratoriae Liber XII* (Oxford, 1948), pp. xxvii–xxxi.

12. H. E. Butler, *The Institutio Oratoria of Quintilian* (London, 1921) II, 442, could not find the cross reference in VI,iii,9, but it is probably only to VI,iii,1. The cross reference in IX,iv,28 to previous "books" seems to apply only to VIII,ii,14.

13. See Paul Shorey, *"Physis, Melete, Episteme,"* *Transactions of the American Philological Association*, XL (1909), 185–201.

## Chapter Three

1. On Roman schools, see Aubrey Gwynn, *Roman Education from Cicero to Quintilian* (Oxford, 1926), pp. 11–45 and Marrou, *A History of Education in Antiquity*, pp. 127–313.

2. Suetonius, *On Grammarians* 3.

3. See the remarks of Pseudo-Plutarch, *On the Education of Children* 11.

4. See Marrou (*op. cit supra* n.1), p. 270.

5. *On Clemency* I,16. Cato the Elder would not let a slave punish his son, but apparently did so himself; see Plutarch, *Cato the Elder* 20.

6. See Colson, *M. Fabii Quintiliani Institutio Oratoriae Liber* I, p. 152.

7. The Greek essay *On the Education of Children* (Pseudo-Plutarch) remarks (10) on a need for general education, but says that most subjects should only be tasted, not studied exhaustively. This essay belongs in a Greek tradition which hardly existed at Rome, making philosophy rather than grammar and rhetoric the heart of education, but parts relating to primary education rather resemble some of Quintilian's teaching.

8. *Letters to His Brother Quintus* III,iii,4.

9. Suetonius, *Augustus* 8 and *Tiberius* 6.

10. *Epistles* V,8.

11. For example, at the beginning of Petronius' *Satyricon*.

12. See V,xiii,36; V,xiii,45–46; VII, ii,54–56.

13. V,xii,17–23. Domitian had prohibited castration, see Suetonius, *Domitian* 7.

14. See Suetonius, *On Grammarians* 25,9 and Cicero, *On the Orator* II, 137–42.

15. This had been suggested long before, see Cicero, *ibid.*, II,99.

16. See Constantin Ritter, *Die Quintilianischen Declamationen: Untersuchungen Über Art und Herkunft* (Freiburg and Tübingen, 1881); A. Trabandt, *De Minoribus Quae Sub Nomine Quintiliani Feruntur Declamationibus* (Griefswald, 1883); Gwynn, (*op. cit supra*, n.1), pp. 209–216.

## Chapter Four

1. The closest to it is *Rhetoric to Herennius*, which has however put the

discussion of style last. Cicero had intended to follow the standard order in *On Invention,* see I,9.

2. Among the passages in which Quintilian disagrees with Cicero are III,ii,4; IV,ii,64; VII,iii,8; IX,i,25; IX, iv,79.

3. See J. Woehrer, "De A. Cornelii Celsi Rhetorica," *Dissertationes Philologiae Vindobonenses,* VII (Vienna and Leipzig, 1903) and Cousin, *passim.*

4. See Michael Winterbottom, "Quintilian and the *Vir Bonus,*" *Journal of Roman Studies,* LIV (1964), 95.

5. *Rhetoric* 1358b. Aristotle says that the audience is either a judge or not. If it is a judge, it judges either past or future. Thus deliberative is a species of judicial, while in Quintilian's system (III,iv,6–7) deliberative is a species of non-judicial oratory.

6. E.g., the advisers to Claudius in Tacitus, *Annals* XII,1–2 or to Galba in *Histories* I,13. The most famous examples, Agrippa and Maecenas to Augustus in Dio Cassius LII, are probably not historical, but the situation seemed plausible to Dio.

7. The Greek *stasis,* plural *staseis,* is now in usage among American speech scholars and is the most sensible technical term, since Latin *status* can lead to confusion. "Base" and "issue" are acceptable translations. On the stasis system, see Dieter Matthes, "Hermagoras von Temnos," *Lustrum,* III (1958), 58–214.

8. Implied in III,vi,67; most explicitly stated in III,vi,82.

9. On the speech of thanks, see Ovid, *Epistles from Pontus* IV,iv,39 and Pliny, *Epistles* II,1 and *Panegyric* 4. On the Capitoline contrast, see Suetonius, *Domitian* 4.

10. III,viii,1; see Cicero, *On the Orator* II,334.

11. See *Anonymous Seguerianus* 26 and Grube (*op. cit supra* chap. II,n.4).

12. IV,i,6–7 and 45–46; see also XI, i,65. The point is lacking in the *Rheto-*

*ric to Herennius* and in Cicero's *On Invention,* and was first suggested in *On the Orator* II,182.

13. See *For Roscius Amerinus* 143.

14. See Asconius' *Commentary on Cicero's For Milo* 31 and 34.

15. *Rhetoric* 1356b.

16. *On Invention* I,57–77.

17. According to Strabo XIII,608–609, most works of Aristotle were lost for about two hundred years, then recovered by Sulla. This was followed by the famous edition of Andronicus and by renewed scholarship among Peripatetics; see Ingmar Düring, *Aristotle in the Ancient Biographical Tradition* (Göteborg, 1957), pp. 412–25. The *Rhetoric* was certainly not very well known to the author of the *Rhetoric to Herennius* or the young Cicero, but they seem to have known of its existence and it probably was not totally lost. Quintilian (II,xvii,15) thought it was available to Critolaus and Athenodorus in the second century. On Quintilian's own knowledge of it, see chap V,n.9.

18. V,xi,5. to VIII,iii,72. On this subject I am indebted to an unpublished Harvard Ph.D. thesis by Marsh McCall, "Ancient Rhetorical Concepts of Simile and Comparison" (1965), chap. VII.

19. See above, chap. III,n.13.

20. VI,i,7, see also II,xvi,4 and X,i, 107; Aristotle, *Rhetoric* 1354a; Athenaeus, *Deipnosophists* XIII,590.

21. *On the Orator* II,183–85.

22. See *On the Orator* II,189.

23. See F. Kuehert, "Quintilians Eröterung über den Witz," *Philologus,* CVI (1962), 29–59 and 305–314.

24. II,216–90.

25. See Jules Humbert, *Les plaidoyers écrits et les plaidoires réalles de Cicéron* (Paris, 1925).

26. Cousin, I,349, remarks on how frequently Quintilian refers to himself in this chapter.

27. III,37.

28. See Kennedy, *The Art of Persuasion in Greece,* pp. 272–78.

29. When Quintilian discusses propriety (*proprietas*) in Book VIII, he means the literal or "proper" use of a word as opposed to some kind of metaphor or abuse. This is quite distinct from the propriety of style discussed in Book XI, usually referred to by the adverb *apte* or the participle *accommodata.*

30. See *On the Orator* III,153.

31. The use of *perspicuus* seems rather arbitrary, but it carries a slightly passive quality, whereas *clare* and *evidenter* are more active.

32. *Rhetoric* 1405a.

33. The presence or absence of *ut* ("as") is not regarded as crucial, see VIII,vi,9 compared with VIII,vi,68–69 and McCall (*op. cit. supra* n.18), p. 289.

34. See Quintilian's reference to Celsus in IX,i,18. Rutilius Lupus and Seneca the Elder simply use *schema* as a Latin word.

35. *On the Arrangement of Words* 8.

36. See E. Ofenloch, *Caecilii Calactini Fragmenta* (Leipzig, 1907), pp. 32–62.

37. See IX,i,36; IX,ii,1; IX,iii,90.

38. *Orator* 181: rhythm, composition, kind of words.

39. Among best known studies are those of Theodor Zielinski, see especially *Der Constructive Rhythmus in Ciceros Reden* (Leipzig, 1914). See also *Oxford Classical Dictionary* (Oxford, 1949), *s.v.* "Prose-rhythm."

40. See *Orator* 216.

41. E.g., IX,iv,97; 98; 99; 102; 105.

42. See *Orator* 217.

43. See IX,iv,36; 40; 108; 109.

44. See *Orator* 192 and 215.

45. See Cousin, I,535–36.

46. See Joseph Gladisch, *De Clausulis Quintilianeis* (Breslau, 1909).

47. See Cicero, *Orator* 222–23.

48. See *On the Orator* III,210.

49. See above. p. 000.

50. See Kennedy (*op. cit. supra,* n. 28), pp. 282–84.

51. *Rhetoric to Herennius* III, 19–27.

52. *On the Orator* III,213–27; *Orator* 55.

53. On the orator's gestures in art, see Richard Brilliant, *Gesture and Rank in Roman Art: the Use of Gestures to Denote Status in Roman Sculpture and Coinage* (New Haven, 1963).

*Chapter Five*

1. See *Odes* III,i,3 and *Epistles* II, i,126–38.

2. The reference to Cremutius (X,i, 104) is dependent on an emendation of the text, but is doubtless correct. Quintilian says portions of the text were suppressed. According to Tacitus *Annals* IV,34–35, the senate tried to please the emperor by ordering Cremutius' work burned, but copies were secretly preserved.

3. See *On the Orator* II,51–64.

4. Note that oratory occupies a less conspicuous position in the order followed than does epic, history, or philosophy. The concept of epic is metrical rather than thematic and is made to include the didactic poetry of Hesiod and the pastoral of Theocritus, which are all in hexameters.

5. See *Brutus* 37 and on the whole subject, the sceptical remarks of A. E. Douglas, "Cicero, Quintilian, and the Canon of Ten Attic Orators," *Mnemosyne,* IX (1956), 30–40.

6. II,51–67 and 93–96.

7. The chief exception is the treatment of tragedy in X,i,66–68.

8. See Hermann Usener, *Dionysii Halicarnassei Librorum De Imitatione Reliquiae* (Bonn, 1889) and Jean Cousin, *Études sur Quintilien,* I,563–73.

9. On Quintilian's knowledge of Aristotle, see Adolphus Roemer, *Aristotelis Ars Rhetorica* (Leipzig, 1898),

pp. lxxxvii–xcii; O. Angermann, *De Aristotele Rhetorum Auctore* (Leipzig, 1904) concluded that Quintilian knew Aristotle only through writers like Caecilius, and many scholars have accepted this judgment. See above chap. IV,n.17.

10. See F. G. Kenyon, *Books and Readers in Ancient Greece and Rome* (Oxford, 1954), chap. III.

11. See Aulus Gellius XV,24.

12. That seems to be what Quintilian means by saying (X,i,86) that Virgil had to work harder than Homer.

13. See Tacitus, *Histories* IV,86.

14. See Valerius Flaccus I,12; Silius Italicus III,620; Statius, *Achilleid* I, 15–16.

15. See G. R. Throop, "Ancient Literary Detractors of Cicero," *Washington University Studies,* I,ii (1913), 19–41.

16. On changes with time, see IX,iii, 1; X,ii,13; XII,x,2. On Cicero's lack of *sententiae,* see XII,x,46.

17. Quintilian as a teacher doubtless took pride in the achievements of his former pupils, but his words go beyond expression of confidence in them. Martial too celebrates the greatness of the age, see *Epigrams* V,19.

18. *Dialogue* 17.

19. See A. D. Leeman, *Orationis Ratio* (Amsterdam, 1963), I,264–83.

20. See Richard McKeon, "Literary Criticism and the Concept of Imitation in Antiquity," *Modern Philology,* XXIV (1936), 1–35; Donald Lemen Clark, *Rhetoric in Greco-Roman Education* (New York, 1957), pp. 144–76; G. M. A. Grube, *The Greek and Roman Critics* (London, 1965), pp. 209–212.

21. *Epistles,* II,iii,291.

22. *Oration* XVIII,18.

23. XXXIV,xix and XXV,xxxiv–xxxvii. See R. G. Austin, "Quintilian on Painting and Statuary," *Classical Quarterly,* XXXVIII (1944), 17–26.

24. *On the Orator* III,26 and *Brutus* 70.

25. *Brutus* 284–291 and *Orator* 23–32; 75–90.

26. Many older editors and translators failed to see that Quintilian praises zeta and upsilon, objects to Latin *f* and consonantal *u;* see R. G. Austin, *Quintiliani Institutionis Oratoriae Liber XII,* pp. 174–80; 237–38.

27. Cicero, *Letters to His Friends* IX,22.

28. On the relation between Quintilian's rules and Pliny's practice, see A. N. Sherwyn-White, *The Letters of Pliny* (Oxford, 1966), pp. 252–53.

29. See Kennedy, *The Art of Persuasion in Greece,* pp. 278–82.

30. See *Orator* 20–21; 70–99.

### Chapter Six

1. See Winterbottom, "Quintilian and the *Vir Bonus,*" 96.

2. See Austin, *Quintiliani Institutionis Oratoriae Liber XII,* pp. xxvii–xxxi.

3. See Dio Cassius LXVII,12. The man was Maternus, and he may have been the same as the Maternus in Tacitus' *Dialogue.* Cicero wants readers of *On the Orator* to remember the fate of its characters, and Tacitus may be doing the same more subtly. Dio calls Maternus a sophist, but this could result from a belief that his offense came in declamation rather than in poetry. Against this view, however, see Alfred Gudeman, *P. Cornelii Taciti Dialogus de Oratoribus* (Leipzig and Berlin, 1914), pp. 38–40.

4. See *On Duties* II,51. Pliny discusses what cases to take in *Epistles,* VI,29.

5. See Tacitus, *Annals* XI,5–7.

6. See Tacitus, *Histories* I,90.

7. See Hans von Arnim, *Dio von Prusa* (Berlin, 1898), p. 134 and Wilbur J. Greer, "Quintilian and the Declamation," *Classical Weekly,* XIX (1925), 27–31. B. Appel, *Das Bildung und Erziehungsideal Ouintilians* (Donauworth, 1914), pp. 27–46, at-

tempts to refute the tie between Quintilian and the second sophistic, but he takes a narrow view, ignoring the often serious purposes and restrained style of some sophists. The best ancient discussion is Philostratus' *Lives of the Sophists*.

8. *Epistles* VI,6.

9. See Dio Cassius LXV,13.

10. On Dio's life see *Oration* XIII and Philostratus, *Lives of the Sophists* 1,7.

11. *Epistles* X,81.

12. See A. M. Guillemin, *Pline et la vie litteraire de son temps* (Paris, 1929) and Leeman, *Orationis Ratio* I, 323–27.

13. See R. Dienel, "Quintilian und der *Rednerdialog* des Tacitus," *Wiener Studien*, XXXVII (1915), 239–71; H. Bardon, "Le *Dialogue des orateurs* et *l'Institution oratoire*," *Revue des Etudes Latines*, XIX (1941), 113–31; R. Guengerich, "Der *Dialogues* des Tacitus und Quintilians *Institutio Oratoria*," *Classical Philology*, XLVI (1951), 159–64; K. Barwick, "Der *Dialogus de Oratoribus* des Tacitus," *Berichte der Akademie der Wissensch. zu Leipzig*, CI,iv (1954); Alain Michel, *Le Dialogue des orateurs de Tacite et la philosophie de Cicéron* (Paris, (1962), pp. 195–96; Leeman (*op. cit. supra*, n.12), I, 320–23.

14. *Dialogue*, 24.

15. *Ibid.*, 30–31.

16. See the works cited in n.13 and Ronald Syme, *Tacitus* (Oxford, 1958), I, 100–111 and II, 670–73.

17. *Agricola* 3.

18. See Winterbottom (*op. cit. supra*, n.1), 91–94.

19. The best discussion in English is that in Colson, *M. Fabii Quintiliani Institutionis Oratoriae Liber* I, pp. xliv–lxxxix.

20. See *Epistles* II,14; VI,6.

21. VI,75; 280; VII,186–189.

22. We know it existed from the index, which survives.

23. See the *Augustan Histories*, XXX *Tyrants*, 4.

24. On the orator-statesman of late antiquity, see Samuel Dill, *Roman Society in the Last Century of the Western Empire* (London, 1921), pp. 425–44 and Terrot R. Glover, *Life and Literature in the Fourth Century* (New York, 1924).

25. Servatus Lupus of Ferrieres (died *ca*.860) complains of the incomplete nature of his text (Migne, *Patrologia Latina*, CXIX, pp. 526 and 579); see Colson (*op. cit supra*, n.19), p. xlix.

26. See Colson (*op. cit supra*, n.19), p. lxxiii.

# Selected Bibliography

PRIMARY SOURCES

*Editions of the Latin Text*

RADERMACHER, LUDWIG. *M. Fabi Quintiliani Institutionis Oratoriae Libri XII*. 1st ed., Leipzig: Teubner, vol. I, 1907; vol. II, 1935; addenda et corrigenda collegit et adiecit *Vinzenz Buchheit*, 2 vols. Leipzig: Teubner, 1959. Though not completely satisfactory, this remains the standard text pending the publication of one in the *Oxford Classical Texts*.

GAUNT, DAVID M. *M. Fabii Quintiliani Institutio Oratoria: Selections from the Latin Text with Digest of the Intervening Material* (with English commentary) London: William Heinemann, 1957.

COLSON, F. H. *M. Fabii Quintiliani Institutionis Oratoriae Liber I* (with English commentary) Cambridge: University Press, 1924.

ADAMIETZ, JOACHIM, *M. F. Quintiliani Institutionis Oratoriae Liber III* (with German commentary). Munich: Wilhelm Fink Verlag, 1966.

PETERSON, W. *Quintiliani Institutionis Oratoriae Liber X* (with English commenary). Oxford: The Clarendon Press, 1st ed., 1891; abridged 2nd ed., 1902 and later.

AUSTIN, R. G. *Quintiliani Institutionis Oratoriae Liber XII* (with English commentary). Oxford: The Clarendon Press, 1948 and later.

*Translations and Summaries*

WATSON, JOHN SELBY. *Quintilian's Institutes of Oratory.* ("Bohn's Classical Library,") 2 vols. London: George Bell, 1856 and later. Books I and II, i–x have been reissued with introduction and notes by JAMES J. MURPHY under the title *On the Early Education of the Citizen-Orator*, Idianapolis: Bobbs-Merrill Co., 1965.

BUTLER, H. E. *The Institutio Oratoria of Quintilian.* ("Loeb Classical Library.") 4 vols. London: William Heinemann; Cambridge, Mass.: Harvard University Press, 1920–22 and later.

SMAIL, WILLIAM M. *Quintilian on Education.* Oxford: The Clarendon Press, 1938. Portions of books I, II, and XII.

LITTLE, CHARLES EDGAR. *The Institutio Oratoria of Marcus Fabius Quintilianus with an English Summary and Concordance.* 2 vols. Nashville: George Peabody College for Teachers, 1951.

SECONDARY SOURCES

APPEL, B. *Das Bildungs- und Erziehungsideal Quintilians nach der Institutio Oratoria.* Donauworth: Ludwig Auer, 1914. Standard discussion of Quintilian's educational goal.

COUSIN, JEAN. *Études sur Quintilien.* 2 vols. Paris: Bowin et Cie, 1936;

reprint, Amsterdam: P. Schippeus N.V., 1967. The first volume is a vast but superficial chapter-by-chapter survey of Quintilian's sources. The second is a lexicon of Greek rhetorical terms.

GABLER, X. *De Elocutione M. F. Quintiliani.* Borna-Leipzig: Robert Noske, 1910. Standard work on Quintilian's own prose style.

GRUBE, G. M. A. *The Greek and Roman Critics.* London: Methuen, 1965. The best history of ancient criticism, with a chapter on Quintilian.

GWYNN, AUBREY. *Roman Education from Cicero to Quintilian.* Oxford: Clarendon Press, 1926. Generally sensible account of Quintilian's educational antecedents.

LEEMAN, A. D. *Orationis Ratio: the Stylistic Theories and Practice of the Roman Orators, Historians, and Philosophers.* 2 vols. Amsterdam: A. M. Hakkert, 1963. History of Latin prose through examination of key writers, including Quintilian.

SAINTSBURY, GEORGE. *A History of Criticism and Literary Taste in Europe from the Earliest Times to the Present Day.* 3 vols. Edinburgh and London: W. Blackwood & Sons, 1900 and later. Book II, chap. iii of this elegant classic is a perceptive essay on Quintilian.

SCHWABE, L. VON. "M. Fabius (137) Quintilianus," *Paulys Real Encyclopädie der classischen Altertumswissenschaft* VI, 2 (Stuttgart: J. B. Metzler, 1909), coll. 1845–1864. Standard scholarly examination of Quintilian's life and works.

WINTERBOTTOM, MICHAEL. "Quintilian and the *Vir Bonus*," *Journal of Roman Studies,* LIV (1964), 90–97. Important article on Quintilian's relationship to the oratory of his time.

## Additional Bibliography

See the editions of Colson and Austin and the work of Cousin cited above. Cousin brought his listings up to date in "Quintilian 1935–1959," *Lustrum,* VII (1963), 289–331.

# Index

Aesop, 45
Afer, see Domitius Afer
Agricola, Rudolph, 140
Alcaeus, 104
Alexander the Great, 14, 52, 60, 132
allegory, 84
amplification, 29, 82–83
analogy, 44
Anaxagoras, 126
anticipation, 72
Antigonus, 118
antithesis, 89
antonomasia, 84
Apollodoreans, 32, 55, 57, 64
Aratus, 108
archaism, 81
argument, 68–70, 95
Aristarchus, 106
Aristeides, 60
Aristophanes of Byzantium, 106
Aristotle, 13, 32, 58, 59, 63, 66, 68, 70,
    72, 73, 74, 77, 80, 83, 89, 90, 92, 98,
    107, 123, 130, 132, 145
arithmetic, 40, 45
arrangement of a speech, 13, 35, 36, 77,
    95, 103, 115
arrangement of words, see composition
Asianism, 92, 119–20
Asinius Pollio, 80
astronomy, 13, 40, 45–46
athletics, 13, 46
Atticism, 89, 118–20
Augustus, 15, 48, 132
Ausonius, 15

Berenice, 21
Brutus, 119

Caecilius, 86, 107

Caelius, 16
Calagurris, 15, 18, 19
Caligula, see Gaius
Calvus, 119
canon of orators, 106
Capito, 16
Capitoline games, 23, 27, 63
Cassiodorus, 139
Cassius Severus, 57
catachresis, 84
Cato the Elder, 14, 34, 73, 124, 130
Catullus, 108
Celsus, 32, 55, 63, 65, 80, 86, 130
character, see ethos
characters of style, 121–22
Charmadas, 96
Chrysippus, 32, 41, 58
Cicero, Marcus, 12, 15, 16, 17, 20, 31,
    47, 48, 49, 59, 60, 61, 63, 65, 68, 69,
    72, 73, 79, 81, 83, 86, 88, 91, 94, 96,
    98, 105, 106, 108, 110–12, 114, 115,
    116, 118, 119, 120, 121, 123, 125,
    126, 128, 130, 131, 135, 136, 137;
    *Against Vatinius*, 66; *Against Verres*,
    95; *Brutus*, 15, 106; *For Caelius*, 95;
    *For Milo*, 64; *On Duties*, 95, 123; *On
    Invention*, 15, 68; *On the Orator*, 15,
    46, 55, 75, 76, 80, 86–87, 96, 106,
    123; *The Orator*, 15, 34, 55, 86–87,
    89–90, 92–93
Cicero, Quintus, 48
classicism, 20, 114, 135
Claudius, 17, 128
clausula, 91–93
Cleanthes, 32, 58
coinage of words, 81, 84
"colors," 65
commonplaces, 47, 66, 69–70, 73, 102
comparison, 70–71

# Index